the BIG BOOK of air AND space flight ACTIVITIES

Jani Macari Pallis

McGraw-Hill
New York San Francisco Washington, D.C. Auckland Bogotá
Caracas Lisbon London Madrid Mexico City Milan
Montreal New Delhi San Juan Singapore
Sydney Tokyo Toronto

ACKNOWLEDGMENTS

This work was supported under NASA cooperative agreement NCC2-9010 awarded to our corporation, Cislunar Aerospace, Inc. (CAI). The constant support of the individuals from the NASA Ames Research Center made this work possible. They are: Mark León, Jill Willard, Christiy Budenbender, and Pat Kaspar.

Many sincerest thanks to the original co-investigators on the project: Juanita Ryan, Janet Meizel, and Patricia Hogan, as well as the original team of educators: Barbara Alden, Heather Banks, Gail Chaid, Laurie Coates, Elaine Dependahl, Theresa Durnin-Chaid, Terry Hawkins, Janet Herman, Julie Shultz, and Linda Swan, and our colleagues from the University of California at Davis: Joan Gargano and Ken Weiss.

Special thanks to my colleague, Dr. F. Carroll Dougherty, Assistant Professor of Mechanical Engineering at the University of South Alabama for her authoring of the fundamentals, propulsion, stability, and control and structures sections.

Robert Clarno did a wonderful job of editing the educator's version of the text into grade-appropriate language. As well, my long-time friend, Gary Hunter, contributed his skills in this area early in the project.

My thanks to my colleagues at CAI, past and present, that critiqued and wrote segments of the materials: Eric Chattot, Dr. David Kinney, Judi Licata, Kevin Okamoto, and Tom Olsen. My personal appreciation to Dave Banks for his review of all of the materials. Special thanks are due to Chad Okamoto, our graphic artist, who made this book and on-line version of the text come alive. His beautiful illustrations added a special dimension to the materials.

I want to thank all the people that I worked with from McGraw-Hill: Mary Loebig Giles, Griffin Hansbury, Paula Jo Smith, Pattie Amoroso, and Clare Stanley. You were all so wonderful to work with!

Finally, to my wonderful husband, Jim, for all the kindness and patience he has demonstrated throughout the development of this work. This book is dedicated to our friend Pat Ryan. We hope it inspires you to follow your dreams!

October 12, 1999
Jani Macari Pallis, Ph.D.
Cislunar Aerospace, Inc.
Napa, California

McGraw-Hill

A Division of The **McGraw-Hill** *Companies*

1 2 3 4 5 6 7 8 9 0 QPD/QPD 9 0 9 8 7 6 5 4 3 2 1 0 9

ISBN 0-07-134820-4

The sponsoring editor for this book was Griffin Hansbury, the editing supervisor was Patricia V. Amoroso, and the production supervisor was Clare B. Stanley. It was set in Gill Sans.

Printed and bound by Quebecor/Dubuque

Photos on pages of the space shuttle, SR-71, F-16, and CV-990 courtesy of NASA Dryden Flight Research Center.

This book is printed on recycled, acid-free paper containing a minimum of 50% recycled de-inked paper.

CONTENTS

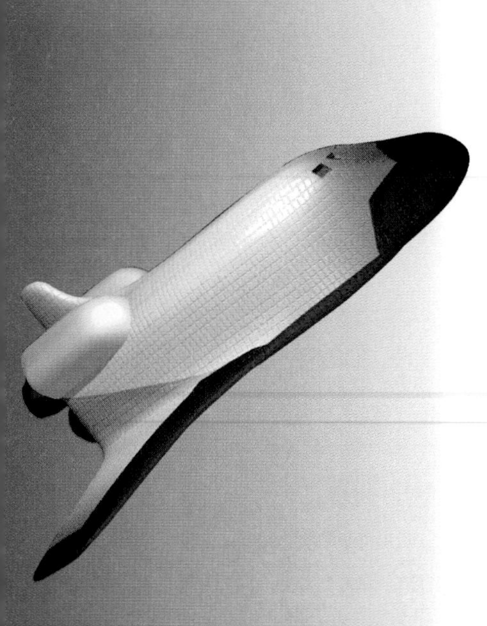

Preface

Do you ever dream about being able to fly or wonder why both birds and planes can fly with such different kinds of wings? Maybe you wonder why some pitched baseballs curve and others drop, why some race cars have "spoilers" on the back or why some swimmers are faster than others. Whether you like flying, racing, swimming, watching animals, or just looking at the clouds passing overhead, there is always some aspect of flight—or "aeronautics"—involved.

We share your curiosity and excitement about how the forces of nature affect our everyday lives. In this book the authors show you how the same principles that keep airplanes in the air are also at work in other areas of our lives. People in the past had to make up stories and myths to explain how things in nature work. As you learn more about the laws of nature, you gain understanding and power. You no longer need these stories to answer your questions.

In this book you will find information about how powered flight developed from early attempts to fly, how water and air move over objects, and what forces affect flight. You will learn about jets and rockets, about how controls move airplanes in different directions, and how structures and materials affect airplane design. We hope you are as excited as we are about this book. It is filled with lively and interesting information, fascinating pictures, and many fun activities you can do on your own. You may even find a pathway toward a career you never dreamed of!

This book is the printed version of the World Wide Web K-8 Aeronautics Internet Textbook (K8AIT). If you have a computer and an Internet connection, you can find even more information about flight from the Web site at http://wings.ucdavis.edu. The online book has still pictures, movie clips, a Spanish-language edition, and sign language for the deaf.

Your teachers will also enjoy this book. They will find intermediate or advanced step-by-step lesson plans and activities that are far more than just another set of plans or "fun" activities—they move from one aspect of aeronautics to the next as a natural part of physical life and earth sciences. Whether you like math, language, social studies, literature, or performing arts, your teacher can find a "curriculum bridge" to a topic you like.

The book was originally developed under a National Aeronautics and Space Administration (NASA) solicitation through NASA's Learning Technologies Project. NASA has a long-standing commitment to communicating science and encouraging students to pursue careers in science, engineering, and technology. NASA's support during the early years of this project made it possible for the authors to put together lesson plans, vocabulary, and activities that not only meet the requirements of the national science framework, but also reach out to Spanish-speaking students, schools for the profoundly deaf, and distance learning and home-schooling programs. Now that NASA funding has been completed, the proceeds Cislunar Aerospace receives from this book will allow the project to continue and expand.

Mark León, Project Manager
Learning Technologies Project
NASA Ames Research Center

About the Editor
Jani Macari Pallis, Ph.D., is an aeronautical engineer and the founder and CEO of Cislunar Aerospace, Inc., and has worked with NASA to create new uses for technology in education. She is the principal investigator for the NASA-sponsored Internet textbook, wings.ucdavis.edu. Noted for her ability to make difficult science materials and math concepts easy to understand, she has been recognized with awards from NASA and the California Association for Aerospace Education.

CHAPTER 1

The History of Air and Space Flight

From the beginning of time people have dreamed of flying and every culture has myths and stories of humans and gods that could fly. The real science of air and space flight took hundreds of years to develop. Through the efforts of many men and women all over the world, new concepts about flight replaced the myths. It was only when science and math theories were proven through invention that the reality of flight was achieved.

Flight is achieved by combining three basic principles: lift, thrust, and control. This science is called aeronautics. *Lift* is the ability to rise in the air. *Thrust* is the power to move through the air and *control* is the ability to go where you want. Modern air and spacecraft use thousands of sophisticated parts to apply these principles.

In the earliest myths and throughout the history of flight we see men and women using these same principles. The development of air and space flight is the recorded history of men and women understanding, overcoming and conquering these principles. We see the same principles applied

FUN FACT:

✔ According to his brother Orville, two years before their first powered aircraft flight at Kill Devil Hills, while riding a train back to their home in Ohio, Wilbur Wright said in frustration, "Not within a thousand years will man ever fly!"

FUN FACTS

✔ The word "astronaut" comes from the Greek terms "astros" meaning "star" and "nautes" meaning "sailor."

over and over again, in different ways and combinations, from small airplanes to the space shuttle. For example, a *glider* needs lift and control, but has no engine for thrust!

It is fascinating to note how some myths applied aeronautics. In one legend, Alexander of Greece harnessed four large birds to a basket in which he rode. By dangling meat in front of each bird, this way or that, lift and control were achieved.

People attached wings to their bodies to try to fly like birds.

Historic pioneers of "flight" took several different paths. Some used artificial wings attached to their bodies or cloth to make early parachutes. Others made balloons. Still others designed gliders. Each invention included one or more of the principles necessary for successful flight. And with each advancement, true flight—flight that incorporates lift, thrust, and control—became closer to a breathtaking reality. Finally, in 1903, the Wright brothers flew the first powered airplane.

Look at what has happened since then! People take airplane flights every day. Humans have stepped on the moon. Unmanned vehicles explore the other planets in our solar system. Astronauts are working in space! As you begin your exploration of air and space flight with this book, remember this is just the beginning. Working with air and spacecraft could be in your future! Now, let's take a closer look at the history of flight!

Wings and Things

Throughout the early history of flight different people have tried to fly or float to earth from heights. Although some of these tries were successful, many ended in failure. People learn from failure; they see what they did wrong and correct their mistakes. As experience was gained the true nature of flight started to become clearer. With each experiment new things were learned.

One of the first objects created to fly was the arrow. Some of the same principles of flight mentioned earlier apply here—the feathers at the tail end of an arrow help control its flight.

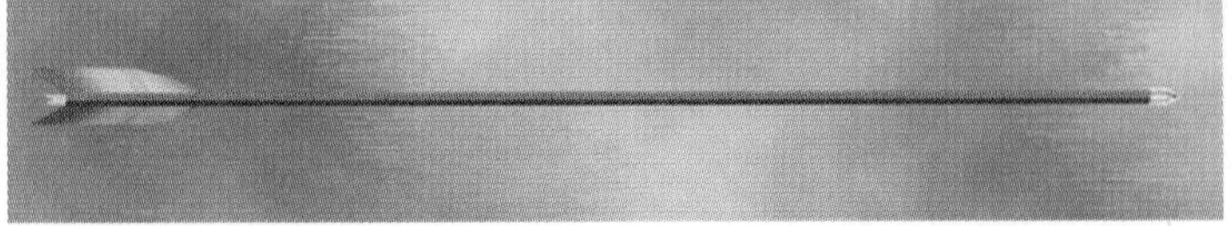

Many people tried to fly by jumping from tall buildings or high mountain tops. In 2200

B.C., the Chinese Emperor Shin jumped from a tower using two large hats. He was very lucky to land safely but did not really fly. He was the first parachutist. But others learned from what he did.

Years passed before the next recorded jump in 852 A. D. Armen Firman jumped from a tower in Spain wearing a huge cloak. He hoped the cloak would billow out and help him float to the ground gently. Fortunately he made it. For many years after, others tried to fly by jumping.

A physician, Abbas ibn-Firmas, covered himself with feathers, attached wings, and flew for some distance. He tried to land like a bird but crashed to the ground, hurting his back. He decided that he failed because he did not have a tail.

In 1678 the first article on attempted flight was published in a French magazine, detailing the experiments of a locksmith named Besnier who had attached wings to his arms and legs. Although unsuccessful, the record of his experiments came to the attention of scientists and inspired discussions that would further the development of *aerodynamic* principles.

In 1797 a Frenchman, Andre-Jacques Garnerin, went up in a hydrogen-filled balloon to 650 feet. He then let himself go in a basket tied to a parachute made of white canvas. He was able to jump, sail down, and land safely on earth. This happened 4000 years after Emperor Shin. Note the advancement from a feathered man jumping to the hydrogen-filled balloon. Lessons were learned with each experiment and contributed to the knowledge of flight. As reports of these experiments were published and read around the world, the ideas accelerated.

BALLOONISTS: Flight Without Wings

During Greek times a great mathematician, Archimedes, discovered the principle of *buoyancy*, helping the progress of flight. He learned that objects dropped in water or air float if they weigh less than the fluid they push aside or displace, and sink if they weigh more. When the great libraries in Alexandria, Egypt, were destroyed in 500 A.D., the discoveries of Archimedes and many others were lost for a thousand years. Two thousand years after Archimedes' discovery, people used the buoyancy principle to build the first hot-air balloon.

One of these people, Roger Bacon, an Englishman, made a balloon-shaped flying machine. He wrote about his invention in the book *The Wonderful Power of Art and Nature* in 1250. The book was so progressive it wasn't published until 1542. The dawning of the Renaissance in 15th-century Italy brought a renewed interest in the arts and sciences. With the invention of movable type by Gutenberg in 1455, new ideas were easily communicated and spread rapidly.

FUN FACTS

✔ A variety of "animalnauts" have flown in space. They include dogs, chimpanzees, rhesus and squirrel monkeys, and even spiders.

In 1648 John Wilkins, a member of the Royal Society of London, was able to replicate the scientific principles of Roger Bacon. But it was two French paper mill owners, the Montgolfier brothers, who built the first hot-air balloon many years later.

In the spring of 1783, Joseph Michel and Jacques Etienne Montgolfier noticed a shirt that had been hung out to dry over a fire. It billowed upward and looked as if it had inflated. They studied the ascending smoke and thought that if they enclosed this "special gas" in an "envelope," the bag would rise from the ground. They experimented with paper bags from their mill over fires made from varying materials. Coining the term "Montgolfier gas," the smoky air created from a fire of straw and wool, they inflated larger and larger balloons. Hot air is lighter than cold air and rises. Filling the balloons with hot air allowed the balloons to rise.

On September 19, 1783, the Montgolfier brothers put a sheep, a duck, and a rooster in a tethered balloon to determine if animals could survive at heights. The experiment took place at the palace at Versailles in France and was witnessed by King Louis XVI, his court, and some 130,000 astonished spectators. The "passengers" were in flight for 8 minutes and traveled almost 2 miles.

A month later, Francois Pilatre de Rozier, a professor of chemistry, went up in another tethered Montgolfier balloon. The balloon was oval shaped, about 49 feet wide and 78 feet high. De Rozier rose to a height of 85 feet. This event is considered to be the first manned lighter-than-air flight.

On November 21, in the same Montgolfier balloon in which the animals had flown, the two-person crew of Rozier and the Marquis d'Arlandes made the first "free flight" (not tethered to the ground). They traveled more than 5 miles across the city of

Paris and reached a height of 3000 feet. D'Arlandes was awed by the view, waving his hat to the open-mouthed spectators below. Suddenly, d'Arlandes noticed that a fire had burned holes in the balloon fabric. D'Arlandes quickly grabbed a sponge and a bucket of water brought along for just such an emergency, and managed to extinguish the fire. After that, the aeronauts found themselves dropping uncomfortably close to the Paris rooftops. They threw more straw on the fire and rose to a more comfortable altitude. Twenty-five minutes after take-off they allowed the fire to subside and landed gently between two mill houses. D'Arlandes wrote later how surprised he was by the silence and the absence of movement among the spectators. Apparently (and rightfully) they were stunned. Practical air travel had begun.

In the same month, Jacques-Alexander Charles, a member of the French Academy of Sciences, made a flight in a balloon filled with hydrogen, which is one-fourteenth the weight of air. The hot-air balloon, which required an open fire, was rather dangerous. Hydrogen, although flammable, was completely enclosed in the balloon before liftoff. In fact the free balloon of today, although it uses noncombustible helium instead of hydrogen, is very similar to the balloon design of Charles. His balloon got up to 3000 feet and traveled about 16 miles in 45 minutes. It was a successful flight, but inspired fear. When the balloon landed, a village man stuck his knife into it. But others saw the value of the flight. Soon the balloon craze broke out across Europe.

FUN FACTS

✔ Benjamin Franklin helped finance Charles's hydrogen balloon flight.

The restrictions of balloon flight were clear—there was no ability to power or control them, so the wind alone determined the flight pattern. The shortcomings of the balloon were recognized as quickly as its success, so many studied to improve its functionality.

Then Henri Giffard, a Frenchman, flew a balloon that used a steam-powered motor. It was able to fly at an average speed of 6.7 MPH. The motor allowed the aeronaut to control the airship. These vehicles were called *dirigibles*. The first fully controllable airship, steerable back to its starting point regardless of wind, was built in 1884 by the team of Charles Renard and A.C. Krebs. It was called "La France" and used an electric power plant and achieved 14.5 MPH.

In 1900 a retired German Cavalry officer, Ferdinand von Zeppelin, used an internal combustion engine to power a dirigible that achieved 18 MPH. It had a rigid metal frame that sustained flight even if gas or power was lost. The gas was evenly distributed into separate compartments, which prevented catastrophe should one compartment fail. By 1910, Zeppelin's airships were reaching speeds of around 40 MPH. The Zeppelin design was copied and improved by others throughout the world. One such airship, the Graf Zeppelin, was three times the length of a Boeing 747 and cruised at 68 MPH. It made regular flights from Europe to South America in which 24 people had their own small bedroom suites and dined from menus prepared by famous chefs. The dirigible was clearly the leader in commercial air travel.

GLIDERS: Fixed Wings

Realizing that lighter-than-air travel was limited, people returned to their study of birds to find the missing link to today's heavier-than-air powered aircraft.

Leonardo da Vinci made the first real studies of flight in 1486. He illustrated his theories on flight in over 150 drawings, but his notebooks were lost until 1797.

George Cayley, an English baronet, realized that people could not fly on their own because they didn't have enough muscle power to create lift. He turned to the kite, an invention from over 2000 years ago, to study lift. Over the next 50 years Cayley improved his principles for controlled gliding flight. Cayley is considered to be the "father of aviation" by many people, and he designed the first *glider*, an engineless flying machine with fixed, nonflapping wings. He studied air pressure and resistance *(drag)* and found the correct position and angle for the wings so that the air flow would lift and stabilize the glider. He found that curved surfaces produced more lift than flat surfaces. He improved *stability* by positioning the tips of the wings higher than the wing roots (the root connects the wing to the rest of the glider).

In 1853, approaching the age of 80, he built a full-size glider and persuaded his coachman to climb on board, then launched the craft from the top of a hill. The glider made a fast swoop across the valley before coming to a sudden halt. The coachman

FUN FACTS

✔ Twelve Americans have walked on the moon since the first lunar landing in 1969. They are : Neil Armstrong, Buzz Aldrin, Pete Conrad, Alan Bean, Alan Shepard, Edgar Mitchell, David Scott, James Irwin, John Young, Charles Duke, Gene Cernan, and Harrison Schmitt.

gave notice immediately upon climbing out that he would no longer be working for his employer in any capacity, but Cayley was thoroughly pleased. He had achieved the first manned heavier-than-air flight in history, and stimulated a great exchange of ideas among those who followed.

The first true airman was Otto Lilienthal, a German engineer and inventor. He was the first person to repeatedly demonstrate that controlled glider flight was possible. His close study of birds contributed many insights as to how they actually fly. He determined, for example, that a bird achieves thrust not simply from the flapping of wings but from the propeller-like action of its primary feathers.

FUN FACTS

✔ Orville and Wilbur Wright's father was a bishop for the Church of the United Brethren in Christ. To respect their father, the sons never flew on Sunday.

In 1891 Lilienthal built and flew the first truly successful glider in history. Gradually modifying his design, he made over 2000 flights in the next 5 years. In 1895 he flew a glider with two sets of wings that lifted with hardly any running start from the 50-foot hill he had constructed, and it carried him distances of a quarter-mile at heights of 75 feet. He planned to attach a motor that would drive a mechanism to flap the wing tips and hopefully extend the duration of his flights.

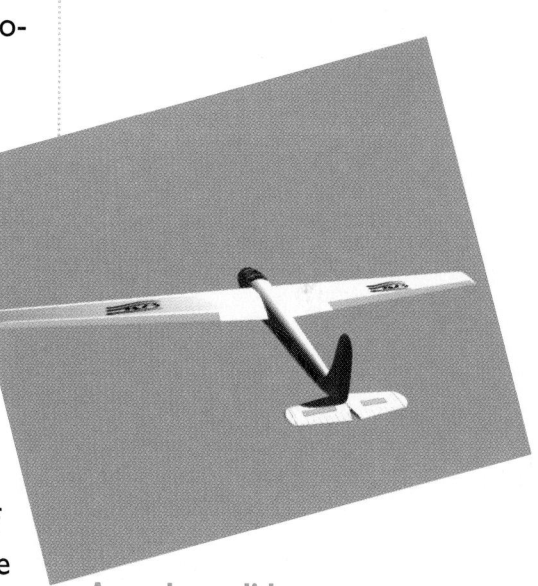

A modern glider.

A drawback to Lilienthal's gliders was that a great deal of control was dependent upon movements of his body. While testing a new design, something failed. Lilienthal fell 50 feet and died the following day, but his achievements had attracted worldwide attention.

POWER AND CONTROL: The Final Ingredients

The earliest recorded use of power to propel an object through the air was during Greek Times. In 1857 Felix du Temple, a French naval officer, designed a powered aeroplane with retractable landing gear. Step by step these new designs furthered the progress of flight.

Another Frenchman, Clement Ader, was the first to lift off the ground in an aircraft with power. But his invention could not be controlled or sustain lift.

Orville and Wilbur Wright became interested in flight as boys in Ohio. Their father gave them a rubber-band-powered toy copter. Although they did not go to college, the brothers were very smart, industrious, and mechanically inclined. When bicycling became popular in the 1890s, the Wright brothers ran a bicycle repair shop and made so much money that they designed and made their own bikes.

FUN FACTS

✔ A dragonfly flaps its two pairs of wings alternately, the front ones rising as the rear ones fall.

The Wrights became seriously interested in aviation when they began reading of Lilienthal's gliding flights in Germany. On May 30, 1899, Wilbur Wright wrote to the Smithsonian Institution in Washington, D.C. He asked if he could obtain papers published by the institution and a list of books in English on the subject of human flight. He received four free pamphlets and a list of five books on the subject. In those days little was written about flight. One book, written by Octave Chanute, inspired the brothers to correspond with the author.

Chanute wrote the Wrights long letters to help them understand the principles of flight.

The Wrights designed a glider much like a kite. They needed strong winds to keep their engineless gliders in the air. Wilbur wrote the Weather Bureau in Washington asking about winds. With the information they received they decided that the winds on the Outer Banks of North Carolina were right for their experiments. Additionally, the water and large sand dunes there would ensure safe landings in case a gliding flight did not go well. They thought about how to steer the aircraft to avoid the problems that had plagued Lilienthal.

FUN FACTS

✔ To have "lift-off" a space vehicle must rise 2 inches. The shortest American flight was achieved by the Mercury-Redstone 1 spacecraft, which flew 4 inches.

They saw a soaring bird right itself from a gust of wind by raising the wing tip of its lowered wing to regain balance. They knew that this technique would give their craft the control needed. They puzzled over how to design this new idea into their vehicle.

One evening at the bicycle shop, Wilbur sold a customer a bicycle tire inner tube. While Wilbur was speaking to the customer, he absent-mindedly started to twist the ends of the long narrow box that had held the inner tube, warping them back and forth in opposite directions. Wilbur realized that he now knew how to imitate the bird's wing! They tested their idea on kites and unmanned gliders before including the "*wing warping*" into their *biplane*.

The Wright brothers began flying gliders near Kitty Hawk, North Carolina, and in over 4 years made 1000 successful gliding flights on those dunes. They agreed with Chanute that control was needed for successful flight. After about a dozen flights in 1900 with a glider of their own design, they changed the shape of the wings and made them larger the next year. They tested their gliders over and over and learned how to launch them and deal with the winds.

In 1901 the Wright brothers met with a lot of failure. The wing design did not create enough lift. They studied *wind tunnels* of other inventors and decided to construct a new one of their own. Wind tunnels are chambers where gas (usually air) is blown over an object to calculate its aerodynamic forces, like lift and drag. The new wind tunnel helped them to improve the redesign of the wing.

In 1902 the Wrights continued with their glider experiments. They were now ready to add the final ingredient: power. During the summer of 1903 they built an airplane named the Flyer that contained a 12-horsepower engine, hand-crafted in their bicycle shop.

On December 14, 1903, they tossed a coin to see who would fly the plane first. Wilbur won. The plane sputtered, dipped on one wing, and crashed into the sand. Repairs were made, and on December 17 it was Orville's turn to fly. The flight lasted only 12 seconds, but it was the first in the history of the world in which a machine carried a man into the air in full flight. Later that same day, Wilbur flew for 59 seconds, covering a distance of 852 feet.

The Age of Flight

The Age of Flight had begun! It would be 5 years before the Wright brothers would get attention for their accomplishment. People just did not believe that the Wrights had succeeded. The Wrights considered uses for their invention in the future—like carrying the mail, passengers, and cargo. The plane could be used in surveillance for the military, to see the movement of the enemy. The brothers also imagined the airplane being used for recreation and in sports. But first they decided to try to interest the military in their invention.

In 1908 the War Department signed a contract for a Wright Flyer if it could pass certain tests. With these tests in 1908, the world finally acknowledged what the Wright brothers had done 5 years earlier.

Soon aerial exhibitions shows became popular. Doubters wanted to see for themselves. People were interested and excited about flying!

> **FUN FACTS**
>
> ✔ Astronaut Alan Shepard was the first person to hit a golf ball on the moon. He said that he hit a "hole-in-one" when the ball landed in a crater.

Airplanes were becoming accepted, and new practical uses for them began to appear. Airplanes could carry goods faster from one city to another than a train could. In 1911 airplanes were used to transport mail. At about the same time, *hydroplanes*, or planes that take off or land on water, were used to carry passengers between San Francisco and Oakland, California, and St. Petersburg and Tampa in Florida. These were the first flights of their kind.

The first flight attendants on an airplane could not be tall because the cabin was not very big, and they were nurses, just in case a passenger became ill.

Aircraft manufacturing techniques were improving as well. Instruments to help pilots fly the airplane were added along with seat belts.

Despite the Wrights inventing the airplane, the United States soon lagged behind European countries in aviation progress. In 1915 President Woodrow Wilson formed the National Advisory Committee on Aeronautics, also known as *NACA*. Later NACA would be renamed *NASA*, the National Aeronautics and Space Administration. NACA's job was to study and make scientific advancements in civil and military aviation, particularly important in light of the fact that World War I was about to begin.

> **FUN FACTS**
>
> ✔ Charles Lindbergh, the first airplane pilot to fly solo across the Atlantic Ocean, helped obtain funding for Goddard's work in rocketry.

Initially airplanes were used to spot artillery, the movement of enemy troops, and to take aerial photographs. Pilots from opposite sides were known to wave at one another. But eventually war led to using the airplane for bombing and aerial combat.

By the end of the war, many advancements made the airplane faster, more powerful, and more reliable. The U. S. Mail Service began using the airplane regularly. Airplanes were also being used in crop dusting and aerial photography in addition to transporting people. The airplane business couldn't be better!

During the 1920s and 1940s more technical advances were made and records were set for long-distance flights, altitude, and speed. Commercial passenger usage was now common.

The motto of flight had become "higher and faster." But how high and how fast? Could humans survive? A series of high-altitude experiments were conducted and people thought of entering space.

Rockets were reported to date as far back as ancient China. When men and women dreamed of flying like birds in the air, just as many dreamed of flying to the stars.

Space flight offered new challenges and problems very different from aviation. An aircraft engine uses the air around it to operate its engine. Oxygen, or an *oxidizer*, is needed to ignite, or combust, the engine's fuel. But in space and on the fringes of space there is little to no air for this process. Rocket engines would have to carry fuel and the oxidizer and deal with more difficult engineering problems.

In the United States, a physics professor, Dr. Robert Goddard, had begun building and experimenting with rockets. In March 1926, in his aunt's orchard, Professor Goddard launched the first successful liquid-propellent rocket. The rocket climbed to 41 feet.

In Europe, the German military became interested in rocketry as well. They invested a tremendous amount of money and personnel into developing a long-range missile named the V-2, an ominous military weapon. Wernher von Braun was one young scientist who worked on the V-2 and dreamed of using rockets for manned space flight. After World War II, Dr. von Braun came to the United States and worked on developing rockets for unmanned and manned space flight.

The United States began developing larger rockets in the late 1940s and tested them at places like White Sands Proving Ground in New Mexico and Cape Canaveral in Florida. In 1955 the United States began working on satellites in the hopes of placing a small *payload* (scientific equipment for taking and transmitting data) of instruments to study the upper atmosphere.

FUN FACTS

- ✔ Astronauts Walter Schirra, Donn Eisele, and Walter Cunningham received a special Emmy award for the first live TV broadcast from space.
- ✔ The phrase "To boldly go where no man has gone before" was spoken by President John F. Kennedy in a speech. He was talking about the future of the space program in the United States.

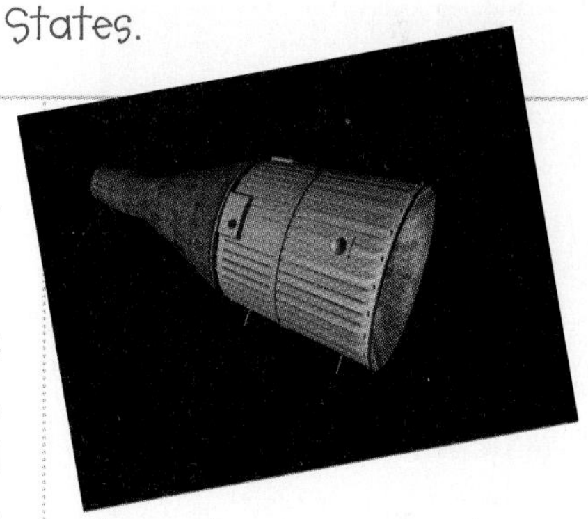

An early space capsule.

But on October 4, 1957, Russia announced the landmark launch of a small satellite into orbit around the earth. The satellite was named "Sputnik," which means "traveling companion" in Russian. Sputnik was less than 2 feet long, but was able to transmit signals back to earth.

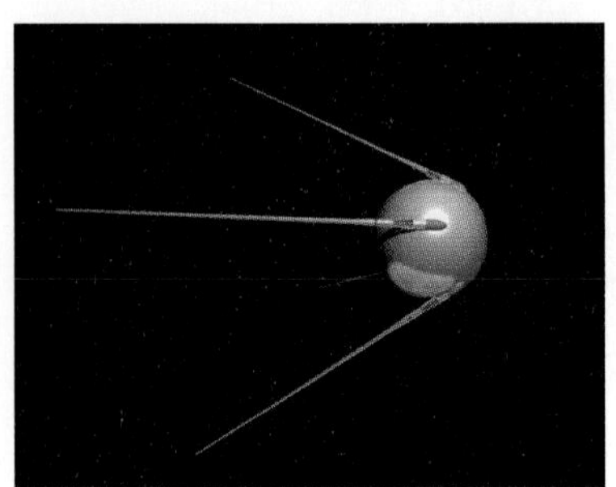

Sputnik—the first satellite launched into orbit around the earth.

Less than a month later Russia sent a second satellite, Sputnik II, into space carrying a dog named "Laika."

The United States launched its own satellite soon after. But the American public was concerned about the Soviet space program. Politicians feared that Soviet superiority in space could threaten national security. In response the American government replaced NACA with NASA—the National Aeronautics and Space Administration—in 1958. One of NASA's missions was to have strong peaceful purposes in the exploration of space.

Much as they had with airplanes, people began realizing the usefulness of satellites. Satellites could help in navigation and weather forecasting as well as observing, collecting, and transmitting information about the earth's atmosphere and space phenomena in addition to information beneficial to national security. Some satellites acted as small telescopes or housed equipment for science experiments.

Satellites are used for weather forecasting, communications, and exploration.

In October 1958, within its first week, NASA announced Project Mercury, the first of three manned space programs for the United States.

In 1961 President John F. Kennedy announced the United States' plans of a mission to the moon. The president promised that U.S. astronauts would land on the moon before the decade was over. And with each project goal achieved, the United States was one step closer to reaching the moon. Other projects in the U.S. space program, like Project Gemini and Project Apollo, contributed to this goal.

Without previous experience in space travel, scientists thought that regular food might "explode" in the low gravity of space. So the first food the early astronauts ate were flavored pastelike substances squeezed from something like toothpaste tubes.

NASA's ultimate goal was to send people to the moon. On July 20, 1969, this dream became reality when Americans Neil Armstrong and Buzz Aldrin stepped onto the moon.

FUN FACTS

✔ The remains of Skylab, the United States' first space station, burned up in the atmosphere and landed in Australia. When a NASA team went to Australia to collect the pieces, the Australian government handed them a ticket for littering.

The purpose of the United States' first space station, Skylab, was to prove that people could live and work in space for an extended period of time. Compared to the Apollo capsule it was spacious, about the size of a small house! The astronauts did not have to wear spacesuits all the time as in previous space capsules. Studies were conducted on how well humans adapted to life in space, and data were collected for earth and solar research. Experiments were also conducted in a field called "microgravity" (very close to no gravity at all). In the absence of gravity, substances behave differently.

Beginning in 1981, a new vehicle called the space shuttle was used for space travel. The shuttle allows men and women to live and work in space. Science experiments conducted on board the shuttle can be used to study the effects of space flight on humans, animals and plants. Other experiments have studied how things can be manufactured in space. The shuttle astronauts also launch satellites from the shuttle and even repair satellites already out in space.

The space station Mir (the Russian word for peace) was occupied by both former Soviet Union and United States crews, demonstrating international cooperation.

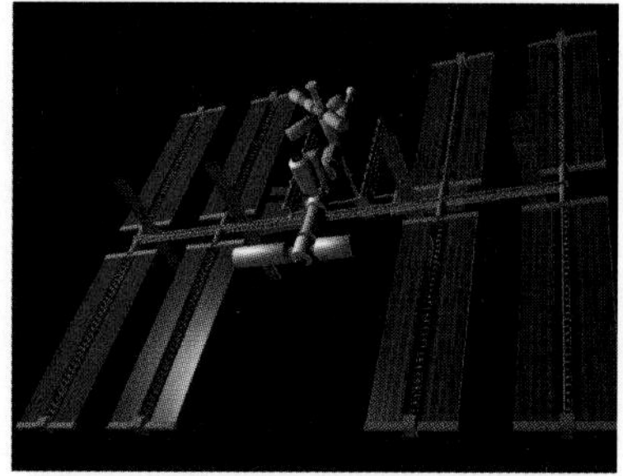
The new International Space Station.

The next endeavor is the International Space Station (ISS). The ISS is the largest scientific collaboration in history—so important and expensive that no one country could create and support it. Sixteen different nations are contributing their scientific expertise and resources to the project. The countries are: the United States, Canada, Brazil, Russia, Belgium, France, Germany, Netherlands, Japan, United Kingdom, Switzerland, Sweden, Spain, Italy, Norway, and Denmark.

Although the station will not be completed until 2004, the first occupants will arrive in January 2000. It will take 45 space missions to build and complete the construction of the station. The first international crew of two Russian cosmonauts and one American astronaut has been training for the mission since 1996. Once on board the station will be continually manned.

The station has over 100 major components. These modules were named by the country which created them. For example, modules from the United States are called "Unity" and "Destiny"; another built by Russia is called "Zarya," which means "Sunrise." Astronauts from all these different countries will live and work in space together in this orbiting laboratory.

2200 BC
China
Emperor Shin
1st Parachute Jump

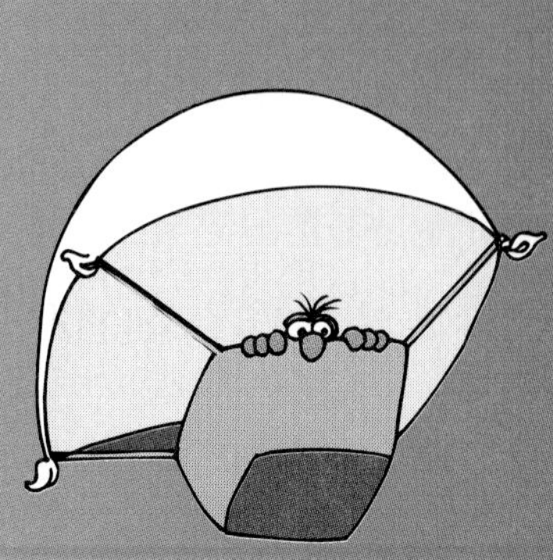

1797
France
Andre-Jacques Garnerin
1st Parachute Jump
from an Air Vehicle

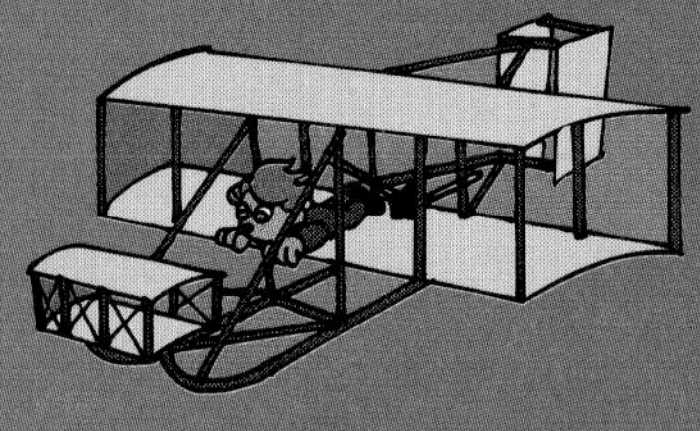

December 17, 1903
USA
Wright Brothers' First
Flight

1783
France
Montgolfier Brothers
1st Manned Lighter-than-air
Flight

1891
Germany
Otto Lilienthal
1st Glider Flight

1908
USA
US War Department
Signs a contract for a Wright Flyer

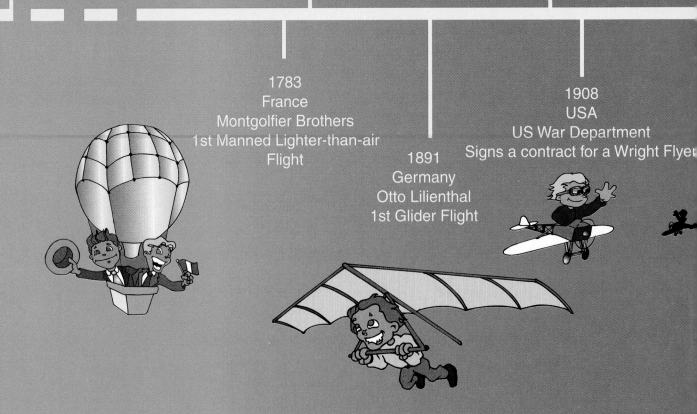

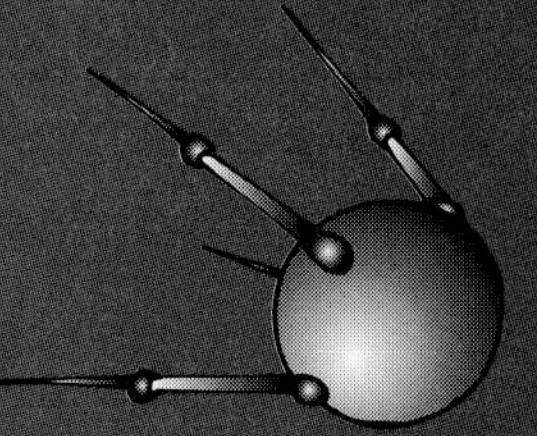

NACA

1915
USA
?resident Woodrow Wilson
formed the
ational Advisory Committee
on Aeronautics

October 4, 1957
Russia
Sputnik
1st Satellite

July 20,1969
Americans Neil Armstrong and
Buzz Aldrin become the 1st men
on the moon

1998
Unity
The International S
began const

March 1926
USA
Professor Goddard
1st Successful Liquid
Propellent Rocket

1958
USA
The NACA becomes NASA.
the National Air and Space
Administration
and Project Mercury
announced

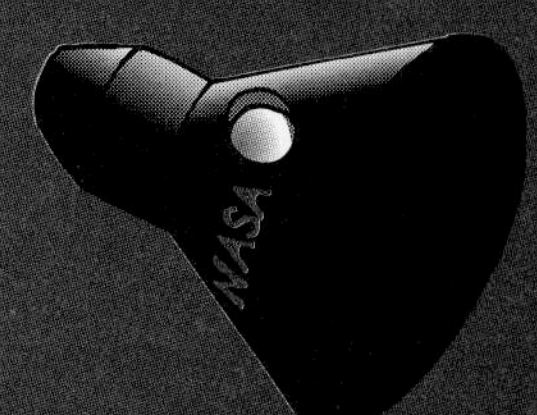

1981
USA
The 1st Space Shutt
Launch

CHAPTER 2

Flight As a Natural Part of Our World

Although mechanical flight has been in existence for less than 100 years, flight in nature has existed for millions of years. Long before humans appeared on this planet, leaves and seeds moved through the air in gliding flight. Later, insects, *ptetosaurs*, birds, and bats achieved true flight.

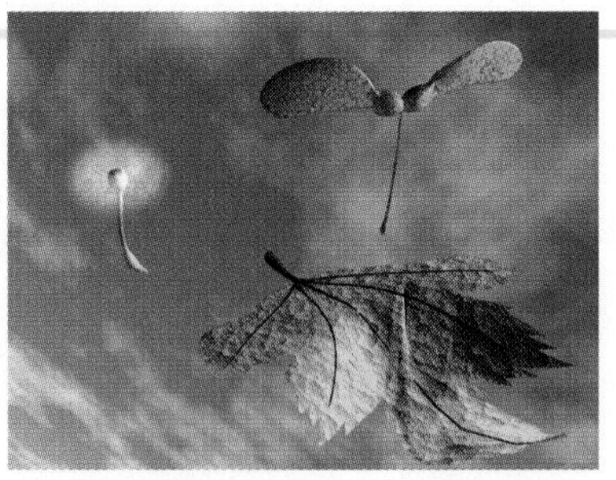

Seeds and leaves float and glide through the air.

Gliding in the Air and Under the Sea

As seeds disperse to find the perfect growing place they seem to "fly" with the wind. Some, like dandelion seeds and milkweed pods, have parachutes made of fine hairs. Other seeds, like maple and ash, have helicopter "wings" that enable them to whirl and sail in the wind over long distances. Seeds and pods are considered gliders and not true flyers because they do not have flapping wings to propel them through the air.

Some amphibians and reptiles, like "flying" frogs, lizards, lemurs, and snakes, can glide through the air. Toe-webbing or extended flaps of abdominal skin create a parachute shape that enable them to glide.

FUN FACTS:

✔ A housefly can somersault in flight to land upside down on a ceiling.

The golden tree snake of the Malayan Peninsula can "glide" from a tree to surprise its prey or an enemy.

Other gliding mammals such as the "flying" squirrels of Asia, North America, and Europe use the furry membrane between their outstretched limbs to "parachute" from tree to tree, using their long tails as rudders for maneuvering.

FUN FACTS

- ✔ While most humans are unable to hear the ultrasonic beeps of bats, some children can.
- ✔ A world altitude record of 37,000 feet was set by a Ruppell's vulture that collided with a commercial aircraft over the Ivory Coast.

Not all animals glide or fly in the air. Many *marine* animals speed under the water. Fast-swimming fish often have special features, like fins that can be tucked away in special grooves when moving quickly, to improve their *streamlining*.

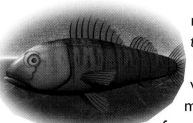

"Flying" fish achieve flightlike movements by means of large *pectoral* fins that serve as wings. When a fish moves through the water it experiences *drag*. For marine life, drag comes in two forms: *pressure drag,* which deals with the body design and streamlining, and *friction drag,* which depends on the surface of the skin. To combat pressure drag, fish have streamlined bodies that move through the water with little resistance.

Fish bodies come in a variety of shapes and sizes which affect the way a fish moves. Fish bodies can be *fusiform* (shaped like torpedoes) like sharks and barracuda, *laterally compressed* (flattened side to side) like angelfish and butterfly fish, *dorsoventrally compressed* (flattened top to bottom) like skates and rays, *attenuated* (slender and tapered) like the moray eel, and any combination of the above.

Some of the fastest fish in the ocean (tuna, mackerel, and jacks) have a somewhat flattened fusiform shape with a reinforced, narrow tail base. Many laterally compressed coral reef fish are very maneuverable, which helps them move in and around the coral.

Other marine life use *jet propulsion* to move freely in the water. The simplest example of this is the jellyfish. These animals fill their umbrella section with water and then push the water out, sending the jellyfish in the opposite direction.

Animals like flying lizards glide rather than fly.

Jellyfish use "jet propulsion" to move under the water.

Several species of two-shelled animals called *bivalves*, such as scallops and clams, also use jet propulsion. To escape a predator, the scallop can rapidly clap its two shells together. Water is forced out between the two shells in jets, sending the scallop to safety. This form of propulsion is very exhausting and cannot be maintained for any length of time. Fortunately, the scallop's predators are slow movers.

True Flight

One of the first ancient flyers was the Pterodactyl.

Although true flyers, some birds, like hawks and vultures, glide and soar to rest their wings and conserve energy. As they glide, they drop lower and lower until finally they must start flapping their wings again to stay up in the air. At other times, they soar higher and higher for hours on warm air currents called *thermals*.

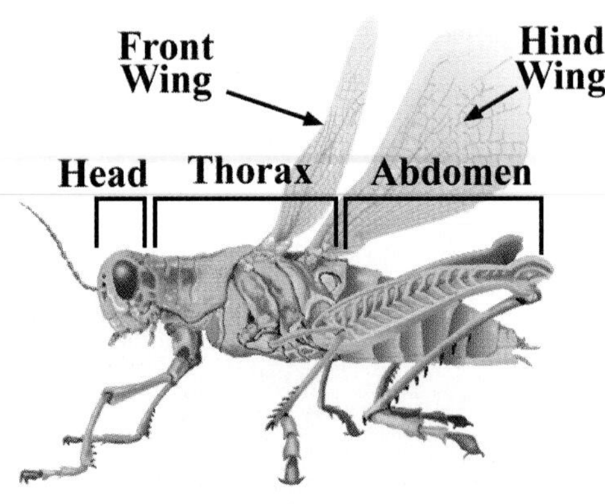

True flight was achieved between 250,000,000 to 65,000,000 years ago by the pterosaurs (Greek for feather-winged lizard). While the most well-known of these ancient flyers is the Pterodactyl, the largest of the pterosaurs was the North American Quetzalcoatlus, with a wingspan of 40 feet from tip to tip. That is as wide as some planes today!

FUN FACTS

✔ Did you know that nine out of ten living things are insects?

Today true flight in nature is accomplished only by insects, birds, and bats, the only animals able to propel themselves through the air for a sustained period of time by flapping their wings.

Insects, the first creatures to develop wings, are the oldest known true flyers. Their tiny but powerful muscles allow most to twist and sway their wings in figure eights, enabling them to fly forward, hover, or even fly backwards.

While insects are considered the most maneuverable of all flying creatures, birds are considered nature's perfect flying machines.

Every part of a bird is adapted to flying. Their bodies are as streamlined as an airplane, enabling them to move easily through the air. Their bones are strong, yet lightweight, because they contain many air sacs. The chest muscle, which operates the wings, is extremely large and powerful. Their wings are covered in tightly fitting feathers that trap air.

Bird feathers have a stiff, straight part running through them called a shaft or a quill. On both sides of the shaft are vanes composed of *barbs* which are held together by *barbules*. The bird's wings, with each of its feathers, are shaped much like an aircraft wing—curved on top and flatter underneath.

The only other animal which flies is the bat. Of the nearly 4000 *mammal* species on earth, bats are the only ones capable of powered flight. As mammals, bats are the only true flyers which nurse their young offspring.

FUN FACTS

- ✔ Most birds fly at low altitudes below 300 feet and only a few dozen species fly higher than 3000 feet.
- ✔ The fastest flying creatures in level flight are ducks and geese, while the peregrine falcon is found to be the fastest when diving from great heights.

Bats belong to the animal order *chiroptera* (Greek for hand-wing). Their wing structure, different from that of birds and insects, is composed of a thin, fleshy membrane stretching from the elongated bones of the forearm to the bat's legs (and sometimes tail). The membrane is supported by elongated finger bones, hence the name "hand-wing." This wing structure enables bats to move their wings much like we move our fingers. As they fly they can flip and turn quickly, often using their wings independently of each other. Like insects, bats are expert acrobatic fliers.

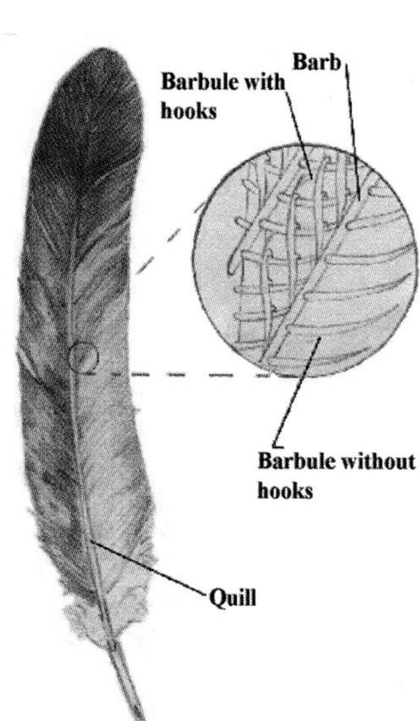

True flight in the natural world is achieved by the presence of wings. But wings, while making these animals similar, also make them unique. As hard as humans tried, they could not imitate animal flight. It was the brain, or intelligence, that eventually enabled people to fly.

Gliding Seeds and Leaves

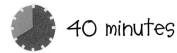

40 minutes

MATERIALS

- an assortment of leaves, petals and seeds
- paper and a pencil or pen
- masking tape (optional)

STEPS TO FOLLOW:

1 Gather an assortment of leaves, petals, and seeds of different shapes and sizes from various plants, flowers, vegetables, and trees. The bigger the assortment, the more fun you will have!

2 With your paper and pencil make a chart. On one side of the paper list or draw the name or shape of the leaves. At the top of the page list some "maneuvers" you will try: toss, drop, twirl.

3 Take your leaves and just toss each, one at a time, into the air. You can do this inside or outside on a windy or calm day. Record on your paper how each leaf behaves. Does it spin around like a discus? Does it glide, float, or just drop to the ground? Note the differences and start to classify or sort them as the leaves fly.

4 Toss a fresh and drier leaf of the same type and size. Do you notice any differences? Does one glide longer than the other?

5 Take two leaves of the same type and size. Remove the stem from one leaf. Now toss them. Do they glide differently? When the leaf touches the ground, which side is facing up? Is it the front (shiny) side of the leaf or the underside of the leaf? Try spinning the leaves; hold each from the tip or from the stem and just let go. Does the leaf twirl like a helicopter?

6 Now take the different leaves, petals, and seeds and build a glider! Use a long leaf for the fuselage (the main body of a glider). Take two leaves with stems and carefully poke a hole on either side of the "fuselage" and thread the stems into the fuselage to make wings. Now fly your "leaf glider."

SCIENCE EXPLANATION:

Gliding seeds and leaves do not use additional energy as they float through the air. Dandelion seeds float like a balloon or a little parachute. Maple leaf seeds twirl like helicopters. Leaves from a maple or fig tree tend to spin like a discus. So your "flight characteristics" will be based on the way the foliage is shaped. Drier leaves have lost part of their moisture and generally glide better because they weigh less.

In making a "leaf glider" you may notice that leaves have a natural curvature to them similar to aircraft wings. You can use this curvature, or "airfoil shape," to your advantage when constructing your leaf glider.

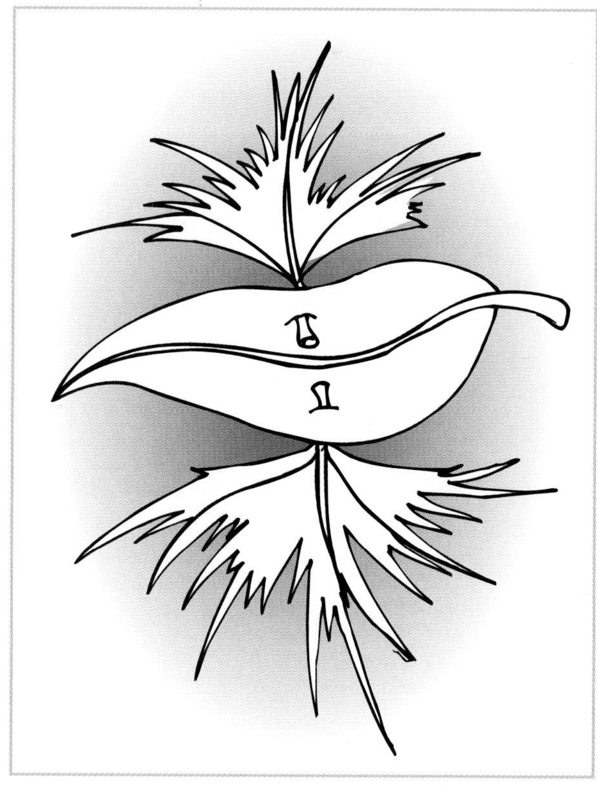

Seed Helicopter

MATERIALS

- 8- 1/2" x 11" paper
- safety scissors
- paper clip
- pattern

STEPS TO FOLLOW:

1 **Copy the pattern onto paper. Cut an 8-1/2" x 11" paper into fourths. Each fourth sheet will make one helicopter.**

2 **Cut the four patterns out. Follow one pattern and cut from A to B. Cut from C to D and from F to E. Fold F to D and C to E. Paper clip the folds together. Now fold down the wings, one forward and the other backward.**

3 **Hold the copter from the short end and then gently let go. The copter should spiral down. Try releasing it from different angles or by holding it differently when you release it. Try to bend or fold up (or down) its different parts. What happens? Does the copter fly differently each time?**

SCIENCE EXPLANATION:

Your seed copter spiraled down, demonstrating its natural gliding flight, much like the leaves and seeds we see in the world around us!

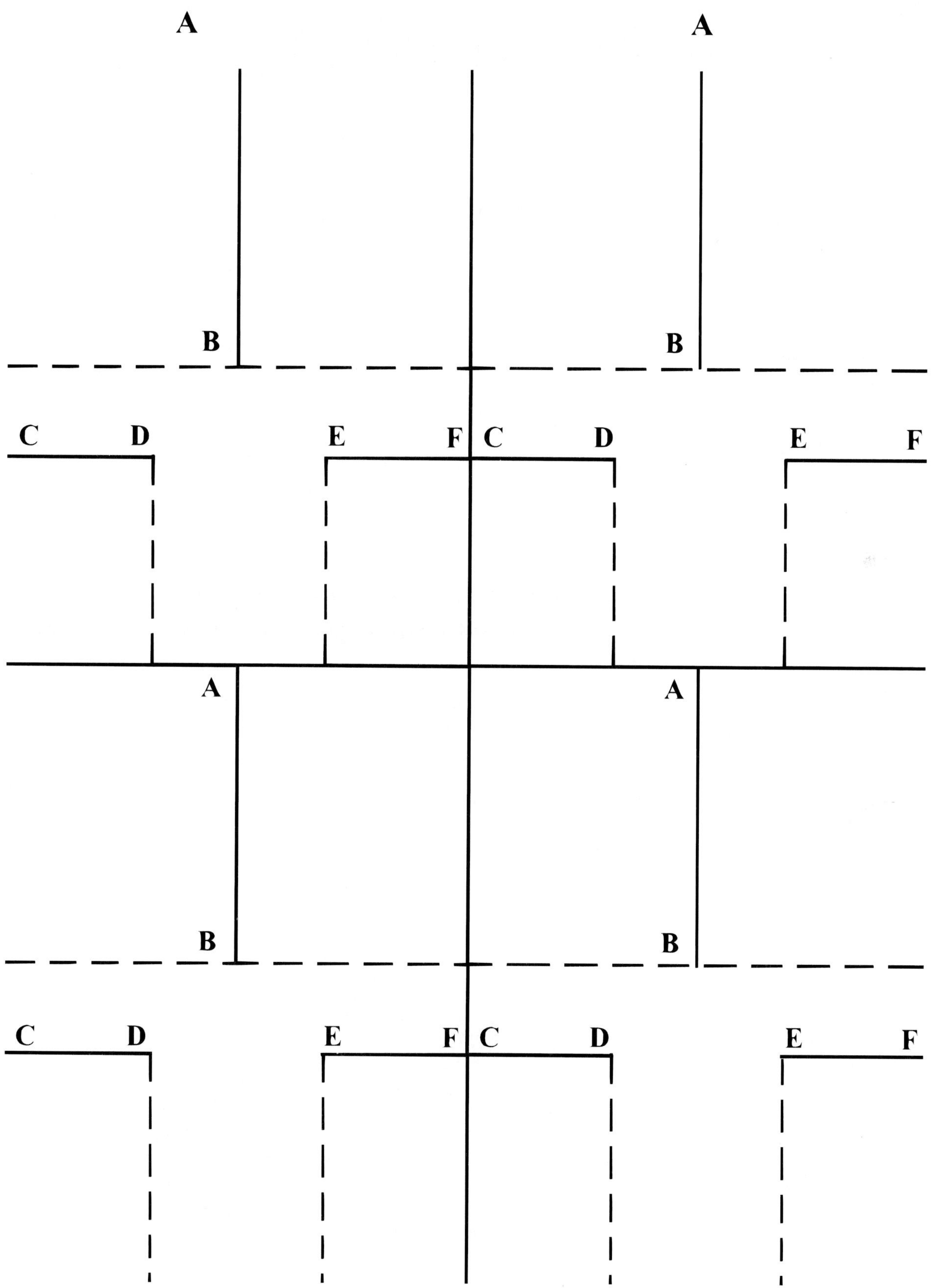
A
A
B
B
C
D
E
F
C
D
E
F
A
A
B
B
C
D
E
F
C
D
E
F

Marine Life

MATERIALS

- pencils
- paper
- fish in a fish tank (you can purchase an aquarium, fish, food, and supplies) or visit someone who has a fish tank—a friend, a pet store, or a local aquarium)

STEPS TO FOLLOW:

1. **Prepare a place where it will be safe to set up an aquarium. Set up the aquarium with the help of an adult. If you don't have an aquarium, and can't set one up, visit a local aquarium, a pet store, or someone you know with a fish tank.**
2. **Watch the fish swimming through the water for several minutes. Look at how their tails, fins, and bodies move.**
3. **How does a fish push through the water? Can a fish turn? How? Can a fish stop? How? Can they swim fast? How do they move up and down in the tank?**
4. **How do the parts of a fish compare to a bird? How do they compare to an airplane?**

SCIENCE EXPLANATION:

Fish are wonderful at moving through the water. Their speed, shape, and body surface as well as the water flow across their body, determine how fish move. Their movement is similar to the gliding of a bird through the air. Fish fins and tails work like bird wings and tails. The same aerodynamic forces are at work only under the sea!

Wing Shapes of Birds and Airplanes

STEPS TO FOLLOW:

1 **Find pictures of birds and airplanes in this book or other books. Look carefully at the wings. How are they similar?**

2 **Pay particular attention to the shape of the wings of certain birds and how airplanes mimic those shapes. Think about how various shapes affect flight patterns.**

3 **Select 3-4 types of birds and airplanes and make comparison drawings of the contours (shapes) of their wings.**

4 **You can also place pictures on an opaque projector, which will project the images onto the wall. Trace the projected images onto construction paper.**

5 **Cut out large-scale silhouettes of the birds and airplanes in flight.**

6 **Fishing line can be threaded through the silhouettes and taped to a hanger to create a mobile. Write the name of the bird or airplane directly onto each silhouette. You may want to group the silhouettes to show the similarities.**

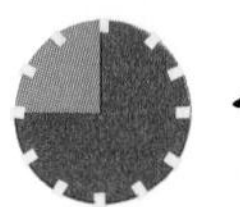

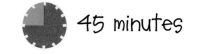

45 minutes

MATERIALS

- pictures of birds and airplanes
- pencils, erasers, and marking pens
- black or colored construction paper (1 sheet for each bird and airplane you draw)
- tracing paper (1 sheet for each bird and airplane you draw)
- 6 –12 inch pieces of clear fishing line (vary the length for each bird or airplane in your mobile)
- clothes hanger
- electrical tape
- opaque projector (optional)

SCIENCE EXPLANATION:

Every part of a bird is adapted for flight and people continue to study these winged creatures to further progress in mechanical flight. The study of bird and aircraft similarities can enhance the understanding of flight patterns. The silhouettes are a practical way to show those similarities.

For example, compare the wing of a bird of prey with a fighter aircraft or the wing of a woodland bird with a stunt aircraft wing. Compare the wing of an albatross to a glider or an eagle's wing to a transport aircraft wing.

CHAPTER 3

The Fundamentals of Flight

Men and women have dreamt of flight for thousands of years. However, it took hundreds of years for humans to understand the *forces* and principles of flight well enough to achieve success.

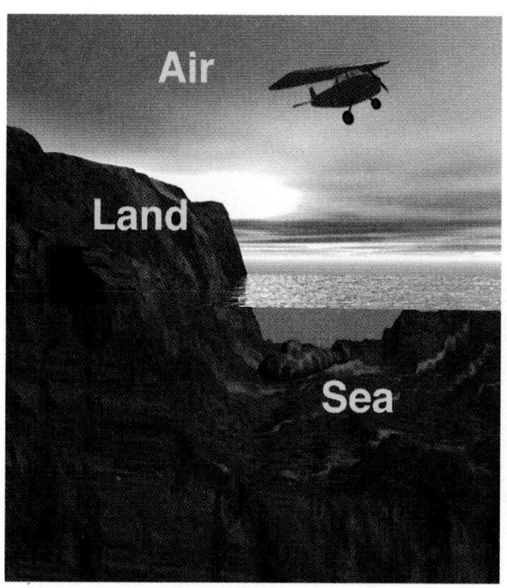

First, humans needed to understand the properties of the earth and air. Men and women invented ways of measuring these elements so that they could be better understood. Over time they developed theories to explain and predict how and why the earth and air behave the way they do. Eventually, humans learned to harness these powers and build the engines and wings to get off the ground and soar with the birds! The science of air flight is called *aeronautics.*

Men and women also dreamed of flight to the stars when they looked up into outer space. The science of space flight is called astronautics.

> **FUN FACTS**
>
> ✔ A boomerang consists of a leading wing and a trailing wing connected at an elbow. As the boomerang flies through the air, each wing produces lift. The spin used in throwing the boomerang stabilizes and curves the flight.

Aeronautics and Aerospace

Aeronautics is the science of flight and also refers to the science of designing an airplane or other flying machine. These are designed by aeronautical engineers.

Aeronautical engineering is not the same as *aerospace* engineering. Aerospace refers to the earth's atmosphere and outer space. Aerospace engineering deals with spacecraft like rockets and satellites. These must ascend through the atmosphere and navigate through space where there is no air. Their designs and engines are different from those of airplanes.

There are four basic subjects that aeronautical and aerospace engineers must understand.

1. ***Aerodynamics***—*How to shape the air or space vehicle so that it can lift itself off the ground and fly easily through the air.*

2. ***Stability and control***—*How to control the vehicle so that it will be able to turn, but not spin out of control.*

3. ***Propulsion***—*How to build an engine (be it propeller, jet, or rocket) so that the vehicle can push its way through the air.*

4. ***Structures***—*How to build the air or spacecraft so that it won't fall apart when it hits a gust of wind; slams down on land, in the water, or on an aircraft carrier; or reenters the earth's atmosphere.*

Additionally, scientists and engineers that work with space vehicles must understand how things work when there is no air and no *gravity*.

To begin, let's look at how air behaves and how scientists and engineers measure things.

How Fluids Move

Most objects on earth or in space can be classified as a solid, a liquid, or a gas. The science of "dynamics" is the study of how these objects behave when there is a force (a push or a pull) acting on it.

Solid objects have well-behaved molecules and atoms that stay together in a pattern and give the object a specific shape. A block of wood and a crystal of salt are solids. A solid has a fixed shape. For example, when a round piece of wood is placed in a square container, its shape does not change to match the container. In dynamics, this is called a "*nondeformable*" body (the shape does not change). No matter how hard a solid is squeezed or pulled, its molecules do not move closer together or farther apart. The object may break, but the molecules don't move. This is an "*incompressible*" object.

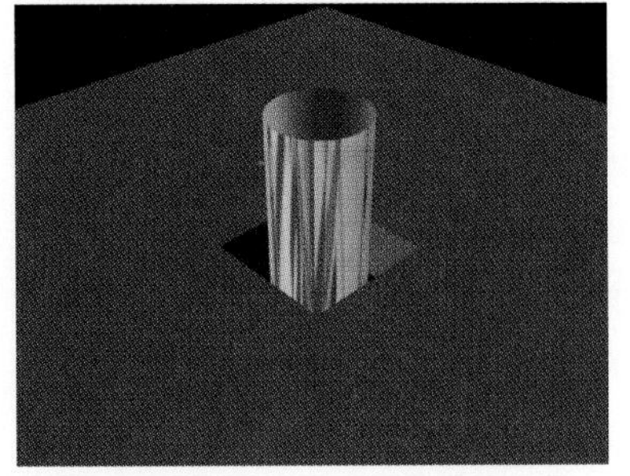

A rounded solid object placed in a square container does not change its shape.

The molecules in a liquid, however, are not so well organized. When poured from a square container into a round one, a liquid will not retain its square shape but will take the shape of the round container. It is *deformable*. The liquid cannot be made larger or smaller by squeezing or pulling. The molecules do not move closer or farther apart. Like the solids, a liquid is incompressible.

Gases, like air, have even less-organized molecules. Gases take the shape of their containers, and also expand or contract to fill the container. When a person breathes air in, for example, the air rushes down the bronchial tubes and tries to fill all the spaces in the lungs. A big breath makes it easier to feel the lungs expand, but a small breath fills ALL of the lungs, too. A gas can be expanded or *compressed*.

Many people use the word "*fluid*" interchangeably with the word "liquid," but scientifically this is not correct. "Fluid" refers to a liquid or a gas. A fluid is deformable.

The study of dynamics can be split into four areas: the dynamics of solids; *hydrodynamics*—or how liquids and other incompressible fluids behave; aerodynamics—how air and other gases move; and *gas dynamics*—how high-speed gases change. Remember, a fluid can be a liquid or a gas. So, "hydrodynamics," "aerodynamics," and "gas dynamics" are all part of a larger area called "*fluid dynamics*," and each will be discussed in the next few pages.

FUN FACTS

- ✔ Drag affects the flight of a golf ball. The dimples help the ball stay in the air longer.
- ✔ The tiny "midge," a gnatlike fly found in swarms around lakes and ponds, beats its wings up to 1000 cycles per second.

Liquids and gases take the shape of their containers. Additionally, gases will contract or expand to fill the container.

How Liquids Behave—Hydrodynamics

Hydrodynamics is the study of how forces (pushes and pulls) affect liquids. Water enables boats or submarines to float. It can move through a pipe or hose or be contained behind a dam. In each case there are rules and laws for the behavior (actions, reactions) of the fluid. Engineers study and apply these rules and laws when they design boats, pipes, dams, or anything that uses a liquid.

How Air Moves

Aerodynamics is the study of the motions and forces of gases on an object. Understanding these forces aids in the design of airplanes, sailboats, cars, and other objects moving quickly through the air as well as buildings, bridges, and windmills affected by the wind moving past them.

Sometimes this is difficult to picture. When we walk through air, we don't really feel anything. Unless there is a wind! Then we feel the force that the air makes on us. Yet, even when there is no wind and we cannot feel the air, it does exert a force on objects.

When air flows over an object at very high speeds, like over a fighter aircraft, or goes through jet engines with very high *temperatures*, the normal rules of aerodynamics sometimes don't apply. Gas dynamics expands the rules and laws of aerodynamics to include these special cases of high speed flows and high temperature flows.

Sometimes, if an aircraft flies very high and very fast, even the rules of gas dynamics break down. At high altitudes air molecules are very far apart. During atmosphere re-entry temperatures around the plane can be so high that they cause chemical reactions among the air molecules. *Hypersonics* is the study of the air motion in these conditions and applies to vehicles like the space shuttle that travel extremely fast.

FUN FACTS

- ✔ A flying fish may soar at speeds of up to 35 miles an hour for distances of 250 yards or more in a single glide!
- ✔ Hypersonic vehicles travel faster than Mach 5—that's faster than a flying bullet. Faster than a mile a second!

Forces in Flight

If you place a book in the palm of your hand and raise your hand over your head, you have applied a force to that book. You "lifted" that book up.

If you and a friend play "tug-of-war" or arm wrestle, each of you are pulling or pushing, trying to win the game. Who will win? The person that can apply the most force.

What if you played "tug-of-war" with three small people pulling against two large people? The group that pulls with the most force will win.

If you get pulled or pushed in many directions, which way will you move? For example, let's say that you are walking into a strong wind and then a friend grabs your hand, trying to pull you to one side. Which way will you go, forward, backward, or to the side? To find out you have to add all of these forces together.

How does this apply to flight? On an air or spacecraft different kinds of forces act on the vehicle at the same time. Which way the vehicle will go depends on the strength of each of these forces. Scientists and engineers have developed methods to quantify these forces and predict which way an object like an airplane will go.

What are the forces that affect the flight of an air or spacecraft and how do we measure them?

FUN FACTS

✔ The majority of astronauts who are scientists graduated from the Massachusetts Institute of Technology.

✔ A cross-section of an airplane's wing is called an "airfoil," while the cross-section of a marine animal's flipper is called a "*hydrofoil*." A sea turtle's flipper resembles an airplane wing and is subjected to the same types of forces when the animal is swimming.

Units

Units are used to define measurements so that everyone knows exactly how much something is. Some examples of units are a meter, a foot, an inch, a centimeter, or a mile. If an engineer designs a bridge and says it is 1000 long and the builder looks at the plans and says it is one short, this is a problem! Are they talking about a meter, a foot, or an inch?

Units measure *mass*, *time*, *length*, and temperature. A measurement should always include two things: a number and a unit. For example, a recipe uses 2 cups of flour; there are 20 minutes until recess; a desk top is 20 inches wide and 25 inches long; it takes 10 days to drive across the country; it is 85 degrees outside today. Note that in each of these examples there is a number and a unit.

Units are used to define measurements. Units measure mass, time, length, and temperature.

Mass

Everything, whether it is a solid, liquid, or gas, has mass. Mass is a measure of how much of the substance is there—how many molecules and what type. Mass is sometimes used interchangeably with *weight* (more on that in the properties section), even though they are not the same. In the metric system, the units for mass are grams (g), kilograms (kg) (1000 grams), or milligrams (mg) (1/1000 grams). In the English system the weight of the substance is used, in pounds or ounces. A pound is 16 ounces.

Time

Time is how long it takes for something to happen. It may take 10 minutes to drive to school; it may take an hour to eat dinner.

The units for time are the same around the world: seconds, hours, days, years. In aerodynamics, a common time measurement is how long it takes an object to go from one point to another or from point A to point B.

Length, Area, and Volume

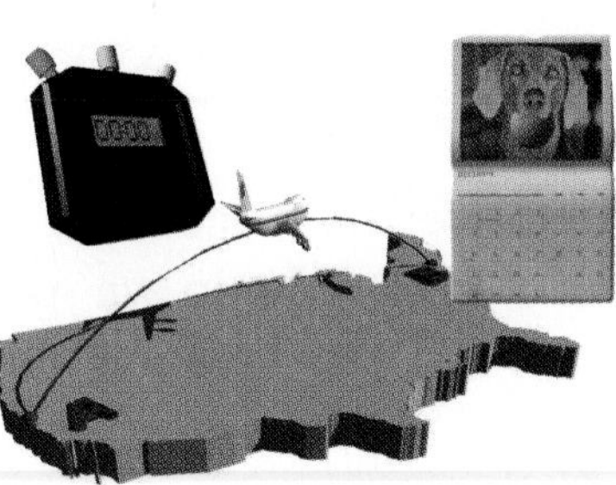

How long is it? How far is it? These are questions heard every day. A pencil is 7 inches long. It is 2 miles to the soccer stadium. A swimming pool is 2 meters deep. The most common length units for the metric system are a centimeter, a meter (100 centimeters), and a kilometer (1000 meters). In the English system that most Americans use, common units are the inch, a foot (12 inches), or a mile (5280 feet).

Area is how much room is on a surface like the floor of the classroom or the surface of a wing. Area is found by multiplying one length by another length and results in "square units." For example, if a room was 20 feet wide by 25 feet long, you would multiply 20 X 25 = 500 square feet.

The *volume* of an object can either be how much space is inside an object, like a fuel tank, or how much actual material is inside a specific place. Volume has three dimensions—length, height, and width (all of these can be called lengths). Multiplying these together equal volume. The result is called a cubic measurement. For example, a 12-inch-long section of a 2 inch by 4 inch board (2 X 4 X 12 inches) would have a volume of 96 cubic inches.

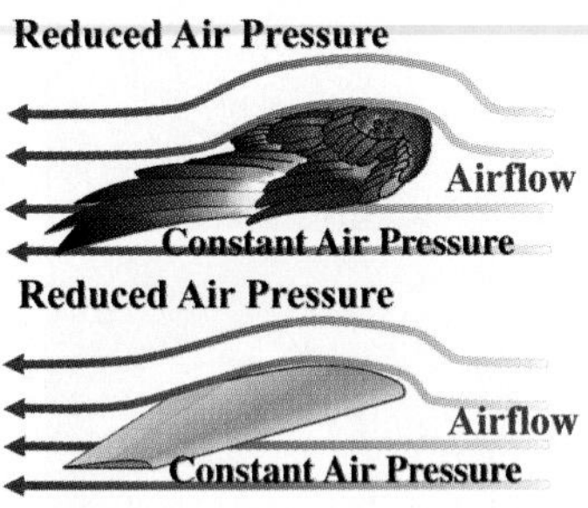

An airplane wing and a bird wing are examples of airfoils. Air flows differently above and below these surfaces.

How Air Moves Over Objects—Aerodynamics

To make air and spacecraft fly you must know how a fluid moves in or around an object. To understand what is happening to a wing, for example, the *aerodynamicist* must know the *velocity* of the plane, its altitude, the size and shape of the wing, and the properties of the air. He or she will need to know how slow- and high-speed air move around the vehicle. An aerodynamicist must pay attention to all of the properties of a fluid (air, water) to understand how a vehicle will fly because all of the properties are linked together.

Let's discuss some of those subjects now!

Temperature

Temperature is a measure of how hot or cold something is. A thermometer is one instrument that determines the temperature of an object. Everything has a temperature—the rocks, trees, people, air. The weather report in the newspaper usually gives the high and low temperatures of the air each day. Common units for temperature are degrees Fahrenheit or degrees Celsius (what used to be called Centigrade). In America, almost everyone uses the Fahrenheit scale. In science and engineering, however, temperatures can be reported using either scale. The way this is shown is either °F or °C.

The temperature of a fluid affects how it behaves. Hot oil, for example, flows faster than cold oil. Warm air rises and cold air drops in a room; house designers often place heat vents at the floor level because of this. Sound travels farther on cold days than hot days.

Common units for temperature are degrees Farenheit or degrees Celsius.

Force

Forces are pushes or pulls on an object. To determine the units of force, scientists and engineers use *Newton's* Second Law of motion which states that a force on a moving object is equal to the mass of the object times the acceleration (a measure of its motion) of the object.

Pressure

Fluid pressure also affects flight. When a fluid moves over or through an object, it gives small pushes on the surface of the object. These pushes, over the entire surface, are defined as pressure and are measured as force per unit area. In metric units, pressure is measured in Newtons per square meter. In the English system, pressure is usually measured in pounds per square inch. Example: The atmosphere (air) presses on your skin at 14.7 pounds per square inch (psi).

Pressure can be powerful. A small pressure, spread over a very large area, can add up to be a very large force. *Air pressure* decreases as altitude increases; pressure also decreases when the speed of the fluid (air, water) increases. When the temperature of a fluid increases, so does the pressure. The pressures on an airplane directly affect its flight capabilities!

Density

Density is a measure of mass (the amount of molecules) in a given object or volume. Density of fluid is measured in kg/cubic meters or lbm/cubic feet.

A fluid with a lot of molecules tightly packed together has a high density; one with fewer molecules would have a lower density. Water, for example, has a much higher density than air. A 10-gallon fish tank with water in it has much more mass than a 10-gallon tank with air in it. Since it has more mass, it will weigh more.

FUN FACTS

✔ The biggest flying bird today is the Great Bustard of Europe and Australia. They weigh as much as 32 pounds, are 4 feet long, and are an endangered species.

Velocity

Velocity is how fast an object moves and is calculated by dividing the distance traveled (a length) by the time it takes to travel the distance. The units of velocity are meters per second (m/s) or feet per minute (ft/min). If a person runs 10 kilometers in 1 hour, his or her velocity is 10 kilometers per hour (km/hr). When engineers work with velocities, they must know the direction and speed of the motion. For example, the rocket traveled upward at a speed of 120 m/s.

Viscosity

Viscosity is a measure of how much a fluid will resist flowing next to a surface. If you spill water on an inclined board, it will run quickly down the board. However, honey spilled on the same board will travel down much more slowly. Honey has a much higher viscosity than water—it is more viscous.

Friction

Friction is resistance to motion, or the force between two objects that rub against one another. The friction between two moving objects can be affected by the surfaces of the objects. For example, it is easier to push a heavy box across a smooth wood floor than it is to push it across thick, bumpy carpet. That means the frictional force between the box and the smooth floor is less than the frictional force between the box and the thick carpet. It takes less of a push to get it moving.

When a fluid like air flows across a surface such as a wing, there is friction resisting the motion. How much friction is dependent on two factors: the viscosity of the fluid and the smoothness of the surface. For example, if water flows across a very rough surface, like a carpet, it will travel down more slowly than on a smooth surface. Because the surface is rougher, the friction force is stronger, the velocity is slower.

Boundary Layer

Because of friction, when a fluid flows over a surface, an interesting pattern develops. The fluid actually stops at the surface. A new layer develops on top of the stopped flow. There is less friction on this new surface and thus a little faster flow. New layers develop, each with less friction, until some distance away from the original surface the remaining layers of the fluid travel at the original velocity. Boundary layers actually control the amount of lift that can be generated.

In general, the *boundary layer* gets thicker as the flow moves along the surface. How fast and how big the boundary layer grows depends on the smoothness and shape of the surface and the velocity of the liquid.

For lower velocities, fluid flowing over a smooth surface that is relatively short and flat will only develop a very thin boundary layer.The flow inside the boundary layer will be smooth and orderly, meaning that the layers will basically stay in layers, without mixing.This is called a *laminar boundary layer.*

As the air or liquid moves over a long, fairly flat surface, the boundary layer gets thicker, and the layers start to mix and swirl around each other. This swirling, rolling layer is called a *turbulent boundary layer*.The mixing and swirling is called *turbulence*; it the swirling is regular and repeatable, it is called a *vortex* or an *eddy*.

Transition

The region in the boundary layer where the orderly laminar layers start to mix together, but before they really start swirling, is called the *transition* region. Most of the time it is a fairly small region.

Flow Separation

When a turbulent boundary really starts to swirl, the boundary layer thickness starts to grow even faster. Eventually, the flow is

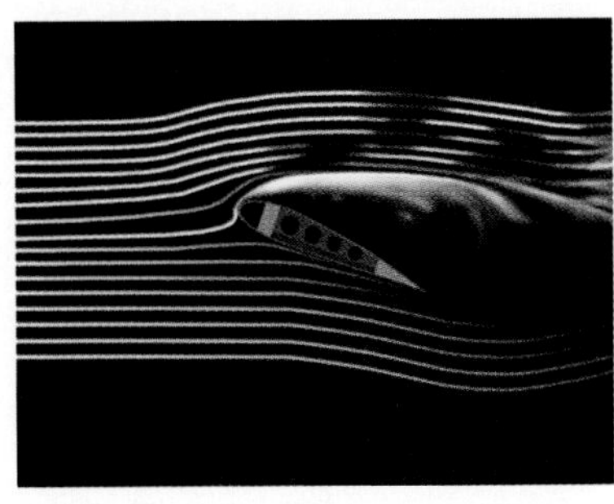

During flow separation the fluid over this airfoil moves over a large bubble.

so mixed, it starts to flow back toward the front of the surface! When this happens, the outside, original fluid is moving over a large bubble created by the turbulence. Inside the bubble, the flow is moving back up the surface. This is called *flow separation*. If the region of flow separation extends past the surface, this region is called a *wake*.

Turbulent boundary layers actually have more energy in them than laminar boundary layers. This means that turbulent boundary layers can keep the flow attached to the wing longer. This is exactly how the dimples on a golf ball work. Originally, golf balls were perfectly smooth. Golfers noticed that used balls that had small dents in them flew longer than smooth balls. Eventually, golf balls were made with dimples.

A stall occurs when the flow separates on a wing. When a wing stalls, the lift (a force that helps a plane to fly) decreases sharply. The plane loses altitude, and if the stall is not corrected, the plane will crash. To land a plane, however, a pilot will wait until the plane is close to the ground, then initiate a slight, controlled stall to gently drop the plane to the runway.

FUN FACTS

✔ The space shuttle creates a sonic boom as it returns to earth through the atmosphere. This is why the shuttle typically lands away from people and buildings. Today, engineers design new space vehicles with sonic boom reduction in mind.

The Speed of Sound

A person standing far from an explosion will not hear it right away. It takes time for the sound waves to travel. These invisible waves of changing pressure move through a fluid (usually air, but sometimes liquid). A person standing closer to the explosion will hear it sooner. At sea level, on a typical day, the *speed of sound* (how fast the sound waves travel) is about 760 miles per hour (MPH). You know that this happens when you see lightning and hear thunder a few seconds later.

Mach Number

The *Mach number* is named for Ernst Mach (1838 -1916), who conducted the first meaningful experiments in *supersonic* flight at the University of Prague, Germany. The numbers Mach 1, Mach 2, Mach 3, etc., are used to show the pilot's speed in comparison to the speed of sound, where Mach 2 is two times the speed of sound.

The way air flows over a wing changes around Mach 1.0. If the speed of the air flow is less then Mach 1.0 it is called *subsonic* flow. Air flow over Mach 1.0 is called supersonic flow. If the Mach number is greater than 5.0, it is called *hypersonic* flow. However, an airplane traveling between Mach 0.75 and Mach 1.20 will have surface areas that are experiencing both subsonic and supersonic airflow; this is called the *transonic* region.

As the plane flies faster than the speed of sound (greater than Mach 1.0), the waves compress into a cone-shaped envelope around the plane. The flow conditions of the air ahead of the plane remain unchanged until the plane flies past. Only the region inside the cone is affected by the plane. This conical compression is called a *shock wave.*

Shocks

In the early days of flight, the aerodynamics of transonic and supersonic flight were not well understood. As pilots flew faster and approached the *sonic* region (called the *sound barrier*, back then) their airplanes would begin to shake and even fall apart! Some people believed that there was an invisible barrier and that humans were not intended to fly faster than the speed of sound.

A conical shock wave forms around the nose of a supersonic vehicle.

In the late 1940s, designers started to understand high-speed aerodynamics and began to build aircraft to fly in the supersonic regime. On October 14, 1947, Captain Charles Yeager flew the first successful supersonic flight in the experimental aircraft Bell XS-1. Today many pilots regularly fly faster than the speed of sound.

As discussed in the Mach number section, when a plane flies faster than the speed of sound, a shock wave is created. This is the cone-shaped area formed around the plane as it flies at supersonic speed or faster. The pressure, density, temperature, and velocity of the air change dramatically and immediately through a shock wave.

Once a shock wave is formed it can travel on and on and on. However, in nature, winds cause the shock to weaken and disperse. When an aircraft flies at supersonic speeds at a high altitude, the shock wave is diffused (scattered) long before it reaches the earth's surface. If a plane flies at supersonic speed too close to the ground, however, the shock hits the earth's surface. This "*sonic boom*" will be heard and felt by observers on the ground. The shock is so strong that it can cause buildings to shake and windows to break!

Bernoulli's Theorem

Daniel Bernoulli (1700-1782) discovered how velocity and pressure change in a fluid: When the velocity in the flow increases, the pressure decreases, and when the velocity decreases, the pressure increases. This theory was vital in designing wings to make flight possible.

Newton's Laws

Sir Isaac Newton developed three laws of physics. These laws help explain air and space flight. Newton's First Law states that a body will remain at rest until acted on by a force. Newton's Second Law defines what a force is. A force is equal to mass times acceleration or F=ma. Newton's Third Law states that for every action there is an equal and opposite reaction. Let's look at how Bernoulli's theorem and Newton's laws help explain why air and spacecraft fly.

Flight Forces

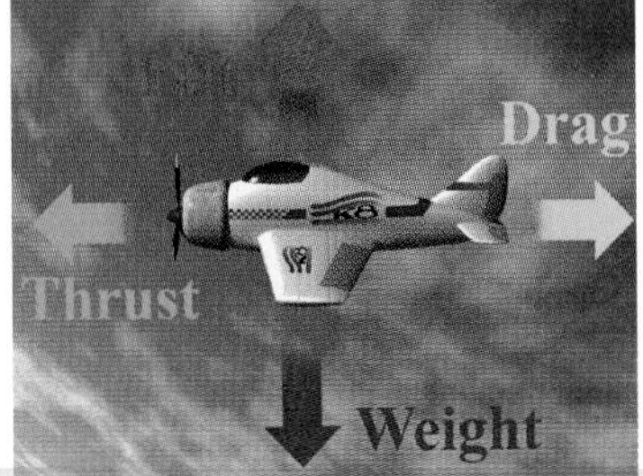

In straight and level flight, the four forces are distributed as shown in the diagram.

The flight of an airplane, a bird, or any other object involves four forces that may be measured and compared: lift, drag, thrust, and weight. As can be seen in the figure to the left, in straight and level flight these four forces are distributed with the 1) lift force pointing upward; 2) weight pushing downward; 3) thrust pointing forward in the direction of flight; and 4) the drag force opposing the thrust. In order for the plane to rise in the air, the lift force must be greater than or equal to the weight. The thrust force must be greater than or equal to the drag force.

Every pilot knows and uses these four basic forces of flight, particularly aerobatic pilots that design amazing stunts to delight the crowds watching them. They deliberately stall the wings of the airplane to cause the plane to lose lift and drop suddenly. They carefully fly upside down, balancing the new lift force with the weight of the plane. They point the airplane straight up and fly as far as they can, let the plane hang there for a second, and then let it fall back down its original path. After a few heartbreaking seconds, the pilot will turn the airplane back so the nose points downward into the direction of the air flow to again regain level flight. These stunts are possible because the pilots carefully balance the forces of weight, lift, drag, and thrust.

Weight and Gravity

In other countries, objects are measured in terms of their mass, in grams or kilograms. In the United States, however, people use the terms for weight to also mean mass. This works okay near the earth's surface because gravity is constant, so the units of weight and mass stay the same. But if an object is taken up high into space, the force of gravity is less. Therefore, the "force" of weight is less.

An object on the moon weighs less than the same object on the earth. The gravitational attraction on the moon is less than that of earth, so the acceleration due to gravity is less (about 1/6th that of the earth). When an object is weighed on the moon, it will weigh about 1/6th as much as the same object on earth. For example, a 60-pound child would weigh 10 pounds on the moon!

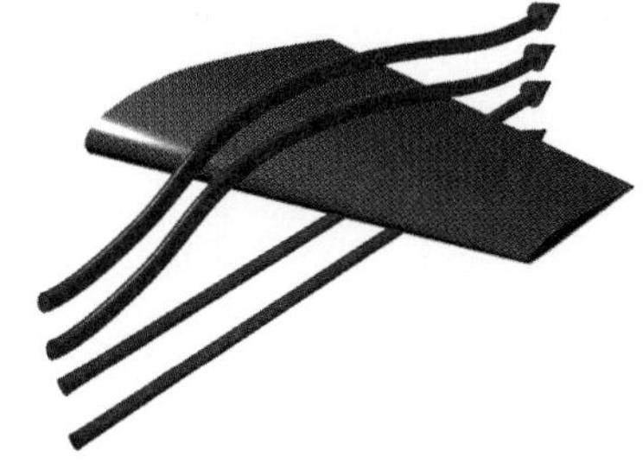

Streamlines travelling above and below a wing.

Lift

The force that pushes an object up against the weight is called lift. On an airplane or a bird, lift is created by the movement of the air around the wings (the lift created by the body or tail is small). The figure shows two streamlines around a typical airfoil (or wing); one travels over the top of the airfoil, the other moves underneath it.

The weight and direction of the aircraft determines how much lift is needed. When accelerating up, lift must be greater than weight. In level flight, lift must equal weight, and accelerating down lift must be less than weight. The minimum speed for lift depends upon the design of the aircraft.

Velocity of the airplane is the most important element in producing lift. If the velocity of the airplane is increased, the lift will increase dramatically. If you double the velocity, you get 4 times the lift; if you triple the speed you get 9 times the lift.

The shape of the airfoil (wing) is important for lift, and is designed carefully. Most airfoils today have camber, or curved upper surfaces and flatter lower surfaces. These airfoils generate lift even when the flow is horizontal (flat). The Wright brothers used *symmetric* airfoils in their airplane design. Since the upper and lower surfaces were the same, the pressures on either surface (top or bottom) are

FUN FACTS

- ✔ The largest bird ever to fly is extinct, but its bones were found in Nevada. Its scientific name is "Teretornis incredibilis," its wing span was 17 feet.
- ✔ Birds have between 1000 and 25,000 feathers, depending upon the species.

the same, so the net combined force on the airfoil is zero and there is no lift! How, then, did the Wright brothers get their airplane off the ground?

To understand the *deflection* of air by an airfoil and how it relates to lift, let's apply Newton's Third Law of Motion. The airfoil deflects the air going over the upper surface downward as it leaves the *trailing edge* of the wing. According to Newton's Third Law, for every action there is an equal, but opposite reaction. Therefore, if the airfoil deflects the air down, the resulting opposite reaction is an upward push. Deflection is an important source of lift. Planes with flat wings, rather than *cambered*, or curved wings, must tilt their wings to deflect the flow.

FUN FACTS

✔ The extinct Moa bird of New Zealand stood 12 feet tall and weighed 700 pounds.

How can you create more lift? A pilot can increase lift by changing the angle of attack, or tilting the leading edge up. This is how the Wright brothers were able to get off the ground. They tilted the wings of their flyer to create lift.

This strategy can be used for either cambered or symmetric wings. This is why an airplane rotates slightly at takeoff; the pilot is increasing the angle of attack to generate more lift. There is a limit to how much lift can be generated, however, and angling too much can result, paradoxically, in a drastic drop of net lift force.

Lift is also used by race car designers who have created airfoil-like surfaces to generate "*negative lift,*" or downward-directed force. This force, combined with the weight of the race car, helps the driver maintain control in the high-speed curves of the race track.

Thrust

Any force pushing an airplane (or bird) forward is called thrust. Thrust is generated by the engines of the airplane (or by the muscles that flap a bird's wings). The engines push fast moving air out behind the plane, by either propeller or jet, causing the plane to move forward.

Drag

Drag is the fourth of the major forces of flight. It is a resistance force and slows the forward motion of an object, including planes. There are four types of drag: friction drag, form drag, induced drag, and *wave drag*. The sum of all four make up the total drag force. The drag forces are the opposite of thrust. If the thrust force is greater than the drag force, the plane goes forward; but if the drag force exceeds the thrust, the plane will slow down and stop.

The friction drag, sometimes called the skin friction drag, is the force created at the surfaces of the plane caused by surface roughness. To minimize friction drag all the sheets of metal on the wing join smoothly, and even the rivets are rounded over and as flush with the surface as possible. Even dead insects and dirt on a wing cause this type of drag.

The form drag, also called pressure drag, is affected by the shape of the body of the airplane. A smooth, streamlined shape will generate less form drag than a blunt or flat body.

Streamlining reduces the form drag of objects that move through fluid. Automobiles are streamlined to increase gas mileage; less drag means less fuel is required to "push" the car forward. Buses and large trucks are less streamlined and heavier, and so require more fuel to move them forward.

FUN FACTS

✔ A Drosphila Fly has been known to fly continuously for 6.5 hours and a Schistocerca Locust for 9 hours.

Induced drag, or drag due to lift, is a small amount of excess (lift) force generated in the direction perpendicular to the lift force along a wing. This force slows the forward motion of the airplane. Aircraft designers try to design wings that lower induced drag.

The last of the four types of drag, wave drag, generally only occurs when an airplane is flying faster than the speed of sound. Wave drag is caused by the interactions of shock waves over the vehicle and the pressure losses due to the shocks. Wave drag can also occur at transonic speeds. Since most commercial jets today fly at transonic speeds, wave drag is an important part of the total drag.

Paper Blow

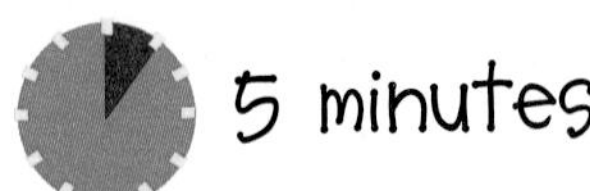

MATERIALS

- one lightweight sheet of notebook-sized paper

STEPS TO FOLLOW:

1. **Hold the sheet of paper by two corners in front of your chin just under your lower lip. (The paper will curve down slightly.)**
2. **Blow steadily under the bottom of the paper. Observe what happens. (The paper lifts.)**
3. **Again, hold the sheet of paper by two corners in front of your chin just under your lower lip. (The paper will curve down slightly.) Blow hard but steadily over the top of the paper. Observe what happens. (The paper lifts.)**

SCIENCE EXPLANATION:

A fluid's molecules are attracted to and attach to a surface. The fast-moving air travels along the paper's surface. One reason that lift occurs is that the pressure on the upper surface on an object (as with many wings) is less than the pressure on the lower surface.

An alternative explanation is Newton's Third Law which states that for every action there is an equal and opposite reaction. The airfoil shape deflected the airflow down at the trailing edge. The equal and opposite reaction was that the paper was lifted into the air.

Paper Tent

STEPS TO FOLLOW:

1 Fold an 8- 1/2 X 11 inch piece of construction paper in half. Tear it in half on the fold making it about 8-1/2 X 5- 1/2 inches. Fold one piece of paper in half to make a paper tent.

2 Place the paper tent on a table or desk. Using the straw, blow under the paper tent. What happens?

3 Now blow hard on the tent and watch what happens.

4 Try blowing hard against the side of the paper tent. What happens?

5 minutes

MATERIALS

- 1 sheet of 8- 1/2 X 11 inch piece of construction paper
- straight drinking straw

SCIENCE EXPLANATION:

The faster air moves, the less pressure it has, so when you blew air through the tent there was less air pressure under the tent than on top of it. The heavy air on top pressed down on the tent causing it to be "sucked" to the table. When you blew on the side of the paper tent you blew it off the table. This same suction occurs on the upper surface of most wings. The top of the wing is curved. Air travels over the wing and moves faster than the air below the wing. The faster air above the wing has less pressure now, and the slower moving air below the wing has more pressure.

Blunt Bodies

Adult supervision is recommended. This experiment requires using a knife.

10 minutes

MATERIALS

- a piece of fruit or a vegetable that does not have a large seed in the middle when cut in half (large apples, small eggplant, large pears work well with this experiment)
- candle stand
- clear plastic tape
- knife
- 2–3 inches of ribbon or paper party streamer

STEPS TO FOLLOW:

1 **Tape the ribbon or paper streamer to the top of the candle stand. Place the fruit or vegetable about 2 inches in front of the candle stand. Blow at the produce and try to make the ribbon or streamer fly. What happens?**

2 **Now place the fruit or vegetable several inches in front of the candle stand. Now try and make the streamers fly. What happens this time?**

3 **Now, have an adult slice the fruit or vegetable in half. Place the piece so that the flat side is facing away from the candle stand and towards you. Try to make the streamers fly as you did with the whole piece of fruit or vegetable. What happens? Where does the air go?**

4 **Now place the candle stand to the side of the piece of fruit or vegetable and blow at the piece. Be sure to place the candle stand only a couple of inches from the apple. What happens now?**

SCIENCE EXPLANATION:

Air flows around various objects and tries to conform to the shape of the object. For flow around the fruit or vegetable, the flow will try to follow the contour of the piece of produce. The air divides into two streams which flow around either side of it. However, the flow cannot negotiate the turn around the rear of the body. The flow will separate on the back side (downstream) of the produce. As the air travels downstream away from the fruit or vegetable, the flow dissipates. So, if the ribbon is close enough to the fruit or vegetable, the ribbon will rise in the air.

When the fruit is sliced in half, the air is still split into two streams, but the air is directed to either side. Since there is a sharp edge, instead of a smooth surface, the air mainly continues in the same direction and the wake is no longer formed behind the apple. However, when the candle stand is moved to the side of the fruit or vegetable, the ribbons will rise in the air again.

Which Way Will It Go?

15 minutes

MATERIALS

- a straight drinking straw
- 2 ping-pong balls
- 1 yard (3 feet) of ribbon or string
- 2 balloons
- 2 8-1/2 X 11 sheets of light-weight paper

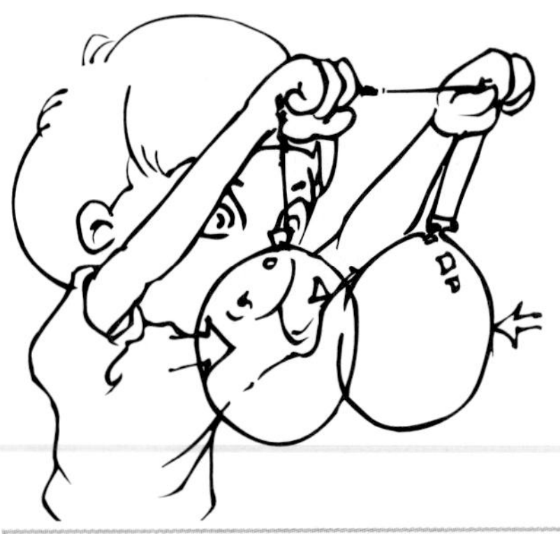

STEPS TO FOLLOW:

1. **Blow up both of the balloons and tie the ends off. Tie one end of the ribbon or string to each balloon.**
2. **Hang the balloons so that they are about 2 inches (5 cm) apart. Blow hard between the two balloons. What happens?**
3. **Next, hold a piece of paper in each hand. Place them in front of your face and hold the two pieces of paper a few inches apart. Blow hard between the two pieces of paper. What happens?**
4. **Last, place the two ping-pong balls on a flat surface near the edge. Place them about 1/2 inch apart from one another. Stoop down so that you can place the straw between but just in front of the ping-ping balls. Blow very hard through the straw. What happens? Which way do the balls move? Closer or farther apart from one another?**

SCIENCE EXPLANATION:

Bernoulli's principle states that when there is an increase in velocity, or air speed, there is a decrease in pressure. The decrease in pressure acts like a small vacuum, sucking the two objects together. The balloons, the papers, and the ping-pong balls all moved closer together and not farther apart as many people would think.

Up in the Air

15 minutes

MATERIALS

- removable self-stick note or a stamp
- a coin (quarter or nickel) or short disc-shaped object (for example, a checker or backgammon piece)
- ping-pong ball

STEPS TO FOLLOW:

1 **If you are using a self-stick note, tear off the sticky part of the note and discard. Place the note or stamp in the palm of one hand.**

2 **Take the coin or disc-shaped object and hold it between the thumb and middle finger. Place it about 1/4 or 1/2 inch above the stamp or piece of paper.**

3 **Place your mouth above the disc or coin and blow hard. The paper should cling to it. Practice! You can really have fun with this. The longer you blow the longer the paper will cling to the object. You should be able to move your hand away and the paper and disc-shaped object should continue to stick together.**

4 **Repeat this experiment again—but this time use a ping pong ball instead of the coin or disc-shaped object. What happens? Can you make the paper cling to the ball? No, the paper blows away.**

SCIENCE EXPLANATION:

Lift occurs when the pressure on the upper surface on an object (wing) is less than the pressure on the lower surface. As the air moves between the paper and the coin or disc-shaped object, a lower pressure area is created. The air pressure below the paper is greater and "holds" it against the coin or disc-shaped object. You were not able to create this situation with the ping-pong ball. Instead, the paper blew farther away.

Drag and Lift

10 minutes

MATERIALS

- 2 pieces of cardboard 20 x 30 inches
- Other size cardboard pieces

STEPS TO FOLLOW:

1. **On a windy day, hold a piece of cardboard so that the wind blows against the flat side. You can feel the large force of drag.**
2. **Next hold the cardboard with the edge facing the wind. In which case is the drag greatest? Do you see any connection between area and drag?**
3. **Now tilt the board and feel the lift.**
4. **Then experiment with different sizes of cardboard. You can also fold a piece of cardboard into different shapes and experiment until they find a shape that resembles an airplane (a shape that seems to offer the least resistance to the wind).**

SCIENCE EXPLANATION:

Aerodynamics is the study of the forces acting on an object due to air, or some other fluid, moving past it. These forces act upon airplanes, sailboats, and other objects moving through the air and affect the motion of those objects.

Lift enables an airplane, or other object, to climb into the air and remain aloft during flight. For example, an object held flat against a stream of air is pushed backward. However, if the object is rotated forward toward the ground, the air can now push it up as well as back.

Wind Tunnel

STEPS TO FOLLOW:

1 Take two of the wrapping paper tubes. Tape them together so that they make one longer tube. Do the same thing for the other six tubes.

2 Stack the tubes together with two tubes across (making two stories). Secure with two long strips of duct tape.

3 Cut out shapes from the Styrofoam. Some should have aerodynamic shapes like an airplane wing and others should be nonaerodynamic (such as a brick shape).

4 Next, turn on the blow dryer and place it in front of the wind tunnel. Tape or secure a plane or shape on the end of a string behind the wind tunnel. Hold it in the airstream behind the wind tunnel.

5 Does the wind current create a lift? (If you try this with a model airplane you can adjust the elevators on the tail assembly which control where the airplane will climb or dive.) What is the position of the elevators in a nose dive? Watch how the air currents affect the lift, turning, rolling, and dive of a plane or shape.

1 hour

MATERIALS

- 8 long wrapping paper tubes
- safety scissors
- a fan or blow dryer
- 6–12 inches of string for each model you test
- duct tape
- long pencils or sticks
- model airplanes, action figure or Styrofoam shapes

SCIENCE EXPLANATION:

A wind tunnel is used by scientists to test model airplanes that have the same shape as actual airplanes. Using the wind tunnel gives the scientists information about how a certain plane would respond in flight.

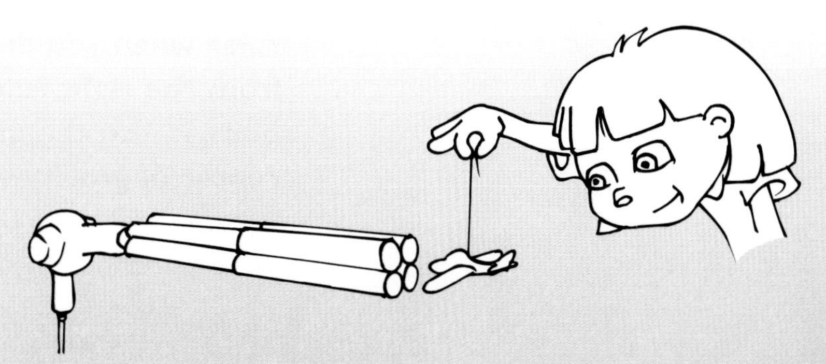

Where Is Your Center of Gravity?

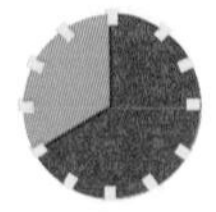

40 minutes

MATERIALS

- 2 bathroom scales
- 1 board (long enough for you to lie on and strong enough to support your weight without bending)
- 2 rulers
- tape measure
- paper and pencils (for writing)

STEPS TO FOLLOW:

1. You will need a partner for part of this experiment. You can take turns with your partner determining each other's center of gravity.
2. Place two bathroom scales on a non-carpeted surface. Check your weight on the bathroom scales. Make sure that you weigh the same on each scale, otherwise adjust the scales accordingly.
3. Lay a ruler horizontally across each scale. Place a board on top of the rulers. The board should be sturdy enough to support you.
4. Read the scales and record the sum of the readings on a piece of paper. This is the weight of the board. Measure the distance between the rulers, which is considered the length of the board. Record this value on your piece of paper.
5. Now lie on the board with the bottom of your feet just above the position of the ruler on the right. Hold your arms by your sides. Have your partner record both scale readings on your paper.
6. Finally, stand against a wall and have your partner measure your height. Record this value on your paper. Since you placed your feet over the right ruler when you did the experiment, **X**, the distance from the right ruler to the center of gravity of the body, is also the distance from your feet to your center of gravity when you are standing.

7 **Subtract 1/2 of the weight of the board from each of your recorded values. Let's call that number from the right scale "RS" and the number from the left scale "LS." Let's call "LBS" the length of the distance between the scales. Your center of gravity is located at the following position on your body measured from your toes: LBS x LS/(LS+RS). That is, multiply the length of the distance between the scales by the reading of the left scale (minus 1/2 the weight of the board) divided by the sum of the reading of the left scale (minus 1/2 the weight of the board) plus the reading of the right scale (minus 1/2 the weight of the board).**

SCIENCE EXPLANATION:

The earth pulls down on each particle of an object with a gravitational force that we call weight. Although individual particles throughout an object all contribute weight in this way, the net effect is as if the total weight of the object were concentrated in a single point—the object's center of gravity.

Friction

MATERIALS

- 4 pieces of wood
- dishwasher soap
- 4 marbles
- 2 pieces of extra heavy aluminum foil; large enough to completely wrap two of the wood blocks

STEPS TO FOLLOW:

1 **Take two of the pieces of wood. Place one on top of the other and lay a hand on the top piece and try to move it. Try and move it by rubbing one piece against the other or using a circular motion. The friction is strong.**

2 **Place a few drops of dishwasher liquid soap between the two pieces of wood and see how well the top piece moves after the lubrication has been applied. Try this using a circular motion. (Be careful when you rub the two pieces together; if you place too much liquid soap between the pieces it can get a bit messy.) What happens?**

3 **Now wrap one of the dry blocks completely in the heavy-duty aluminum foil. Have the ends of the foil meet on the back side of the block. Do the same for the second block. If you do not have heavy-duty aluminum foil you can use a lighter weight foil (but it tends to tear).**

4 **Place one of the aluminum foil blocks on top of the other aluminum foil block. Now repeat the above experiment. Lay a hand on the top piece and try to move it. Try and move it by rubbing one piece against the other or using a circular motion. Can you move the block? How does this feel in comparison to the wood block?**

5 **Now, unwrap one of the aluminum foil covered blocks or use the dry side of one of the wood blocks. Place the four marbles in the palm of one hand. Cup your hand a little bit but keep your hand straight to keep the balls in your hand. Rub the block over the balls. What happens? Does the wood block roll on top of the balls? How does that feel in comparison to the other experiments you did with the blocks of wood?**

SCIENCE EXPLANATION:

We can reduce friction in machines by lubrication. Oil is put into the machine, where it coats surfaces that rub and makes them slippery. All surfaces have tiny projections that catch against each other as they rub. Without lubrication, there would be great friction, slowing and overheating the machine. The oil film separates the two surfaces so that their small rough spots do not catch.

Lubrication is not the only way to reduce friction in machines. Rolling is another way. Placing small steel balls or cylinders between two moving surfaces allows one surface to roll over the ground on wheels. The balls or cylinders do not rub against the surfaces as they roll, so very little friction occurs.

CHAPTER 4

Parts of a Flying Machine

Each part of an air or space vehicle serves a specific purpose—to help lift the vehicle, propel it forward or into space, protect the passengers and cargo, or help the pilot control it. Let's start by taking a look at the structure of a flying machine.

The science of "*structures*" deals with how the plane is built and with what materials. Aircraft structural design is different from other structural fields (such as buildings or ships) because the plane must be both lightweight and strong, able to stay together even through gusts of wind or flying at very high speeds.

For space flight the design must be able to withstand the hostile conditions that occur during launch and re-entry into the atmosphere, like much higher speeds and temperatures. Engineers carefully consider the structure and materials used in spacecraft to ensure that the astronauts can withstand and survive these conditions.

Believe it or not, there is a lot of debris floating around in space. This "space junk" travels very fast and can hit and damage satellites and other space vehicles in its path.

Of the four forces involved in flight—lift, drag, thrust, weight—structure affects the weight. The total weight of the plane is the aircraft itself plus the passengers, crew, baggage and freight, and the fuel. This is called *takeoff weight*. There

FUN FACTS

✔ Bats make up one fourth of all mammal species and are second in diversity only to rodents.

must be enough lift to get the total weight of the airplane into the air. Engineers also consider cruising weight and landing weight—the totals of the empty weight, payload weight, and the weight of the fuel at the time.

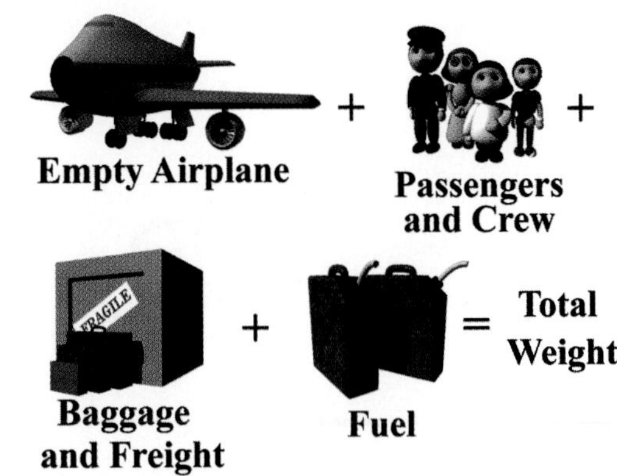

As an airplane gets ready for takeoff several questions must be considered. Will the takeoff weight inhibit the plane from getting off the ground before the end of the runway? Will the distance the plane needs to travel with a heavy payload require more fuel than the plane can carry? Tradeoffs may have to be made: lighter payloads for shorter runways, larger airplanes and heavier payloads with more fuel and longer runways.

FUN FACTS

- ✔ "Bird" is the slang word for a missile or rocket. "Beast" is slang for a very big missile or rocket.
- ✔ Although difficult to measure, the speed of bats has been clocked at up to 75 miles per hour.

In addition to weight, the science of structures deals with strength, the ability of a vehicle to withstand the aerodynamic forces during flight. The aircraft designer builds with two goals in mind—to make the forces on a single part as small as possible so that it will last for a long time and to design all the pieces so that if one fails, the other parts will take on the load. Engineers refer to the first goal as "safe life." Each unit is designed to have as little force as possible on it—lengthening the life of each part beyond the plane's expected life or until scheduled replacement. "Fail safe" is the second goal and means designing the entire air or spacecraft so that failure in one part doesn't cause the whole vehicle to come apart.

Development of Aircraft Structures

Very early airplanes were built from very lightweight materials such as bamboo, wood, and fabric and were designed much like bridges. The wings on the Wright Flyer and other airplanes formed a *truss*. The two wings used wires and bars mounted at an angle to strengthen the wing against aerodynamic forces.

The insides of wings were also a type of truss construction. The inside bars, called *spars*, and wires used on the diagonals,

FUN FACTS

✔ The word aileron comes from the French word for the tips of a bird's wings.

✔ "LOX" is the abbreviation for liquid oxygen. LOX was used as an oxidizer for liquid propellent rockets.

directions. The resulting material is very strong in all directions and very light and stiff, helping to reduce the weight of the airplane structure. However, the materials are very expensive and require a lot of experience to build correctly. As more of these parts are made the experience level will go up and the cost will go down.

Stability and Controls

What Makes It Fly?

Stability for an airplane means that it will resist change in direction and even restore itself to the original course. Control is the science of flying and handling an aircraft. The control engineer makes sure that an aircraft is safe, responds to the controls, and is relatively easy for the pilot to fly.

Another way to think about stability is the ability of the plane to fly itself! The small airplanes used at local airports are very stable, easy to fly, and forgiving of pilot mistakes—perfect for both beginning and more experienced flyers. Commercial aircraft are moderately stable, built to turn smoothly and provide a comfortable ride for passengers, but the pilot must work harder to fly them smoothly. Some military aircraft, especially fighters, are not very stable at all, making them much more difficult to fly. The payoff is that the pilot can *maneuver* the plane very quickly—a critical ability in an aerial dogfight!

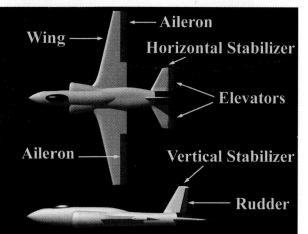

The pilot can change the motion of an airplane by moving the controls. The controls cause changes in one or more of the forces of flight. The pilot uses the control surfaces, such as the *rudder*, *ailerons*, and *elevators*, to change the way forces act on the airplane. The controls impact the plane's direction, speed, and altitude.

History

In the first 10 years of powered flight many people built and were test-flying airplanes. In the United States and Europe these planes were built to be stable and safe, easy to fly, but were difficult to maneuver.

strengthened the wing. The spars and spar caps at each end were shaped to give the wing aerodynamic features. This shape is often called an *airfoil*. The figure to the right shows the basic construction of the wing of the Sopwith Camel, World War I fighter.

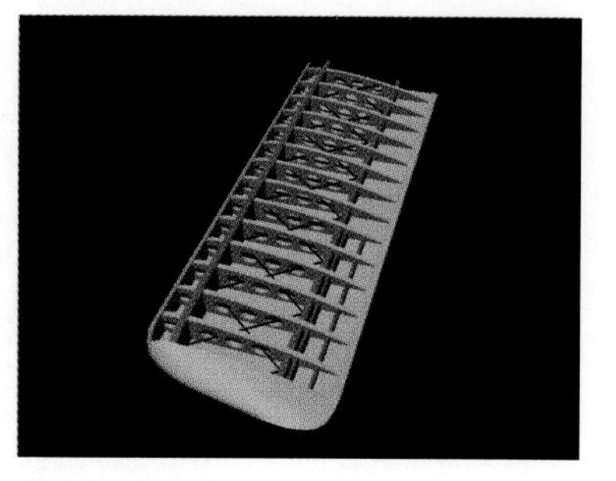

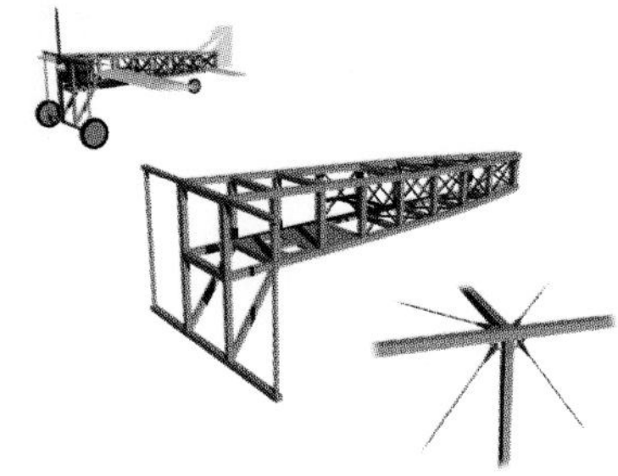

As manufacturing techniques for metals improved in the early 1900s, metal rods and pieces began to replace the wooden components in airplanes. Metal skins, rolled very thin, were used because they withstood weather better than fabric skins. The ribs and spars of the plane were made by riveting many pieces together. When aluminum alloys became available at the end of the 1920s, ribs and spars were often stamped (cut) out of whole aluminum sheets.

When an airplane flies it has stress or loads on its frame. At first, the wood or metal frame took all of the stress. The fabric or thin metal skin was not strong enough to take any of the load. Later, thicker metal skin used on an airplane frame was able to share the stress. Then, the metal frame could be made of lighter metal. The planes weighed less overall!

As more metals were used, the basic design of airplanes changed. The original biplane design with struts and bracing wires was no longer efficient at higher speeds; spars and wires caused more drag and slowed the airplane. Using metal skins to carry some of the load made the biplane design unnecessary and undesirable. Monoplanes, single wing planes without struts and wires sticking out, created much less drag than a biplane.

Design work continues in the field of aircraft structures to look for a better balance of weight and strength. New structural designs are improved by better manufacturing methods and this has produced better structural parts and *alloys*.

Basic Loads

Airplanes are made up of parts or components that experience stress or loads in flight or even while standing still. Tension and *compression stresses* occur when the atoms of a component are being pulled apart or pushed together. Another type of stress, called shear stress, occurs when layers of atoms try to slide across each other sideways. The shear stress can be illustrated by using two blocks of wood nailed together, one on top of the other. If one block of wood was pushed to the right and the other block of wood was pushed to the left, the nails

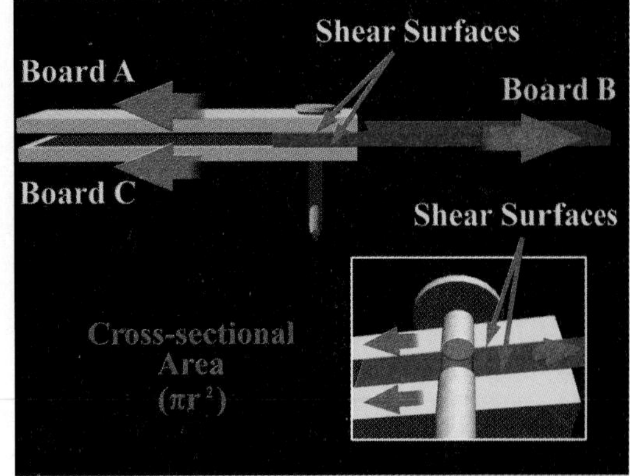

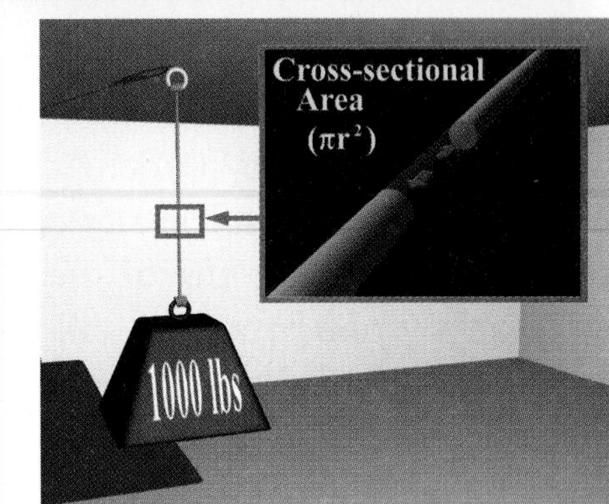

would experience a shear stress at the point where the two blocks of wood meet.

When a component experiences any of the stresses described above, it may deform. For example, a wire hanging from the ceiling with a weight on the end may stretch a little bit because of the weight pulling down on it.

Engineers use a diagram called a stress-strain diagram to predict how much *loading* a component can stand before it fails or breaks. A string of bubble gum can be used for illustration. When a small coin is placed at the bottom of the string of chewed bubble gum, it will stretch a little bit. When the weight is removed the bubble gum will go back to its original length. Heavier weight can be used, and each time the bubble gum will go back to the original length. Eventually, however, the weight will get so heavy that the bubble gum string will not return to its original length but will be permanently stretched. If more weight is added the gum string will break.

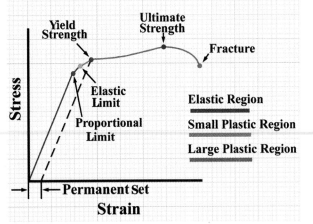

A stress-strain diagram.

The components in an aircraft are not intended to fail or become deformed! The engineer looks at the estimated load or stress and chooses the proper type and size of material needed. Most engineers prefer to design a part with a safety factor built in, so that unexpected loadings from wind gusts and turbulence will not exceed the yield strength of the part.

Elements of Structures

There are three basic types of materials or elements in the structure of an airplane: *stiffened shells, stiffened plates*, and *I-beams*. Stiffening means that the plate or shell has oddly shaped pieces of metal welded to the back side to strengthen it. This allows the plate or shell to carry more weight. On an airplane, the fuselage and *nacelles*, which cover the engine, have stiffened shells. The wing itself can be considered an I-beam. Spars are welded to the I-beam, at right angles, to form the wing. The top and bottom surfaces of the wings are covered with stiffened plates.

Plates and shells tend to be thin. This means they can buckle or bend long before they reach the failure point. For this reason, engineers try to design stiffened shells and plates to prevent permanent deformation. This means much more stress can be applied before bending occurs.

One way to understand buckling is to think of a thin rod standing on end on a solid surface. As more and more weight is placed on top of the rod, it will reach a critical point and bend or buckle. To compute where that critical point is, the engineer must know the strength of the material, *elasticity* or ability to deform, the length, shape, and diameter of the rod.

Materials

Most of the structural components of an airplane are made of metallic materials. An aluminum alloy, used on most metallic components, is relatively lightweight and is strong enough to carry heavy loads. Steel is used for a smaller number of components that are exposed to heavy loads. Landing gears, engine fittings, and the tracks that the flaps move along are usually made of steel. Since aluminum and steel tend to lose their strength at high temperatures, titanium is used around engines, or fireproof walls, known as *firewalls*, to prevent the spread of fire in hot ducts.

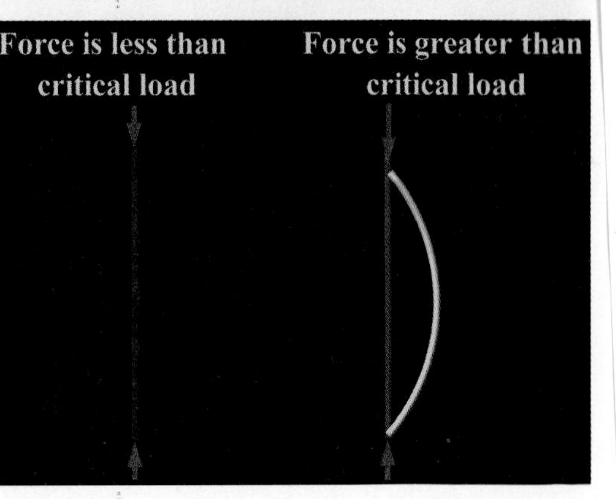

More and more, *composite materials* are being used for some components. Composite materials, made by bonding two or more materials together, are composed of fibers of *boron* or graphite embedded in a layer of *epoxy*. The fibers are very strong in one direction but not in the other. To overcome this problem, most composite materials are created by layering the thin sheets with the fibers in alternating

The Wright brothers, however, designed aircraft that were not very stable. Their goal was to have quick and easy maneuverability, but this required control at every instant of flight. New pilots needed long periods of training in order to fly these difficult and dangerous planes.

On the morning of January 13, 1908, Henri Farman flew his Voisin-Farman biplane on a long, more-or-less circular path around a field in France. The flight lasted 1 minute and 28 seconds and marked the longest flight in Europe at that point. It was also the first circular flight. The Voisin-Farman biplane had only a very basic rudder. Farman had to swing the airplane around by its tail in order to make a long, flat turn. During the turn, the wings remained parallel, or aligned with the ground.

Just seven months later, on August 8, 1908, in another field in France, Wilbur Wright made his first public flight in Europe. He and his brother had been working in secret for years. Aviation pioneers from all over Europe came to see if the rumors about the Wright brothers and their plane were true. Flying the new Wright type A biplane, Wilbur took off, made two graceful circles above the field, and landed after 1 minute and 45 seconds of flight. Using their patented design of twisting the wingtips, called wing warping, Wilbur was able to bank and turn easily. The European aviators were amazed and quickly admitted that the Wright brothers' design was superior.

The European designers quickly adopted the Wright brothers' patented concepts for control using the wing warping and rudders. But, unwilling to give up the idea of a stable aircraft, they expanded on the Wright brothers' plans by adding movable surfaces on the wings near the tips. Using ailerons instead of wing warping kept the desired stability and control. The new designs were able to make the turns that Wilbur had demonstrated so clearly that year, but much more safely and easily. By 1910, the European planes began to surpass the Wright's machines.

The concept of built-in stability for airplane design became the basic feature for all successful aircraft up to the 1970s. Oddly enough, newer designs for fighter aircraft have gone back to the Wright brothers' idea of inherently unstable aircraft. Now, control surfaces on fighter airplanes must again be adjusted at all times. Computers constantly monitor and electronically change the control surfaces, making it less taxing on the pilot.

FUN FACTS

✔ Gray Bats are endangered and live in only nine caves in the United States.

The principle of inherent stability in airplane design is changing because of the increased use of the computer.

Primary Motions

An airplane can move in six different ways—*the six degrees of freedom of motion.* An easy way to demonstrate the motions is to use the right-hand rule. This is a technique or method engineers use to help them define the orientation or position of an object (like an airplane) and the ways it can move. Using the right hand (palm down), extend the thumb to the left. Point the index finger at a right angle to the thumb, so that they are on the same level. Then point the middle finger downward. These are the three axes or centers of motion for the airplane. Think of the airplane with its nose pointing out along the index finger and the wing out along the thumb.

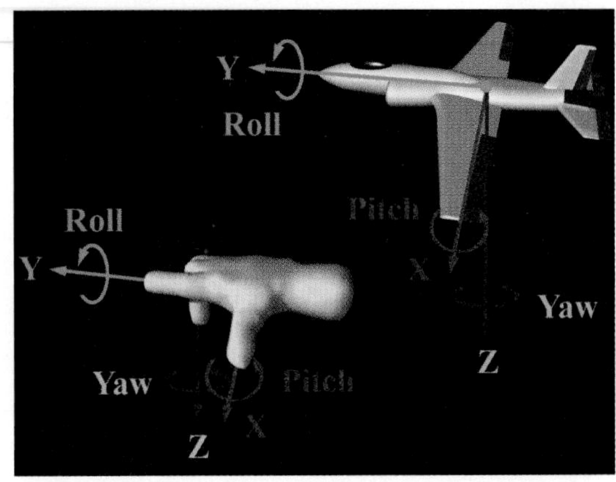

The right-hand rule.

The plane can move forward or backwards along the index finger (the y axis), left or right along the thumb (the x axis), and up or down along the axis of the middle finger (the z axis). These three motions are known as translations or movements along the axes.

FUN FACTS

✔ The names of the first seven astronauts were M. Scott Carpenter, L. Gordon Cooper, John H. Glenn, Virgil I. Grissom, Walter M. Schirra, Alan B. Shepard, and Donald K. Slayton.

Use the handshape above to demonstrate *pitch*, *roll*, and *yaw*. Pitch: Tip the index finger up and down. The index finger represents the nose of the plane. The pitch of the airplane is directly connected to the lift calculation.

Roll: Hold the index finger steady and rotate the hand back and forth. The thumb represents the wings. As it moves up and down it shows how the wings move during a roll.

Yaw: Move the hand from side to side at the wrist. The nose and wings are shown in a sideways motion.

These three rotations—roll, pitch, and yaw—combined with the three translations, define the six degrees of freedom of motion.

Stability

Stability can be static or dynamic. *Static stability* means that when you move an object it returns to its original position. *Dynamic stability* looks at how much time it may take for the object to return to its original position.

Static stability can easily be demonstrated with a marble and a round bowl on a flat surface. Place the marble gently in the bottom of the bowl so that it is not moving. This is the original or *equilibrium position*. If the marble is given a light push in one direction, it will try to return to the center of the bowl, and eventually it will return to the original equilibrium position. This is called a statically stable system. This was the goal of the early airplane designers: that the airplane would try to return to its original orientation after a disturbance, such as a gust of wind.

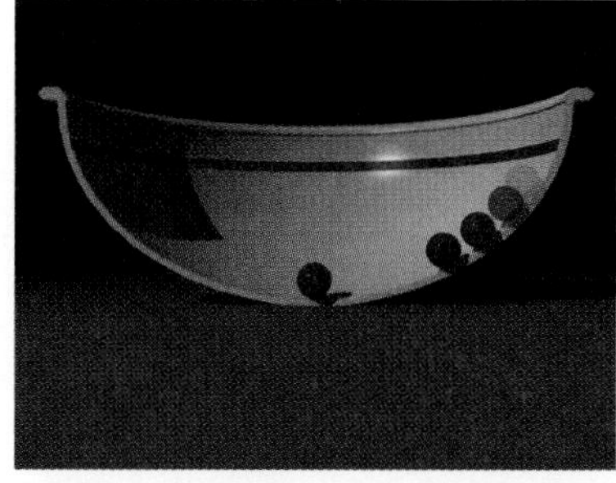

Static stability.

If the bowl is turned over (round bottom up), and the marble placed gently on the top, any slight touch will cause the marble to pick up speed and roll off the bowl. It will not return to its original position! This is called a statically unstable system. Statically unstable airplanes need constant attention to control and keep the airplane on course; otherwise, like the marble, the plane will move any way the forces push it.

Statically unstable.

Dynamic stability is concerned with how long it takes an object to return to its original position. Again, the marble in the bowl can be used to illustrate this concept. Place the marble at the bottom of the bowl. After it is moved slightly, watch how long it takes to come back to its original position. If the object eventually does return to its original position, then the system is considered dynamically stable. If it does not, then it is considered *dynamically unstable*. If the marble is given too much of a push, it could fly out of the bowl and never return to its original position!

Basic Controls

The primary controls the pilot uses are the ailerons, the elevators, and the rudder. The elevators are the horizontal flaps on the tail assembly. Elevators in buildings go up or down. Elevators on the tail assembly cause the nose of the airplane to point up or down. The rudder is the vertical flap on the tail assembly. It helps the airplane turn. The ailerons are the flaps on the trailing edge of the wing. The ailerons help in banking or turning the aircraft. These are shown clearly in the figures at the top of the next page.

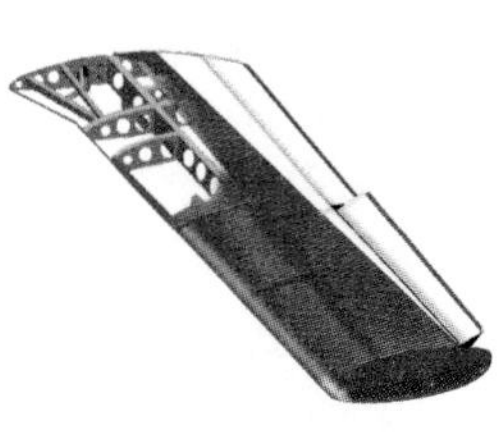

To make a turn, the pilot will move a control device in the cockpit. This is usually either a stick in a fighter-type aircraft or a yoke in most others. The yoke looks similar to a car steering wheel. In making a turn, one aileron goes up and lift decreases. At the same time the other aileron goes down and lift increases. The airplane will roll with the high-lift wing up and lower-lift wing down. If a pilot wishes to turn right, he or she will raise the right aileron and lower the left aileron (by moving the stick or yoke to the right). The right wing will dip as the left wing rotates upward. Rolling the airplane is considered a lateral or sideways motion, so the ailerons are called *lateral controls*.

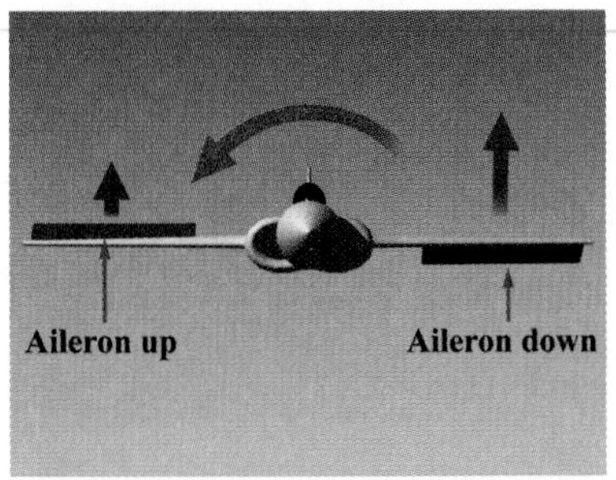

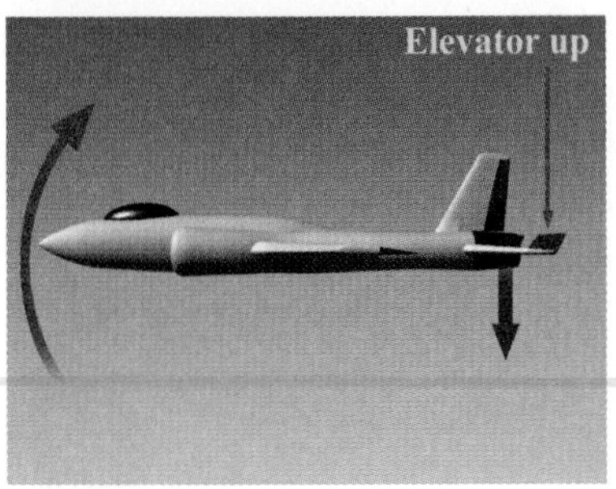

The pilot uses the elevators on the tail to pitch the airplane. This means that if the pilot pulls back on the stick or yoke the elevators move up. The lift on the tail surfaces decrease, causing the nose to pitch up; the opposite happens if the stick or yoke is pushed forward. As the nose and wings pitch up the airflow will increase the overall lift on the plane. The plane will begin to climb. The pitching motion is longitudinal, over the length of the airplane, and so the elevators are known as *longitudinal controls*.

To start a yawing or turning motion, the pilot will use the rudder. Most rudders are controlled by pedals operated by the feet of the pilot. If the pilot steps on the right rudder pedal, the rudder moves to the pilot's right. The pressures on the right side of the rudder are now higher. The plane begins to rotate in a clockwise direction, or to the right! The rudder is called a *directional control*, since yawing is considered a directional motion.

FUN FACTS

✔ Flying Foxes aren't really foxes, but are the largest bats known—with a wing span of up to 6 feet.

Rolling and yawing of the airplane are related; it is very hard to do one without the other. For example, during a right turn, when the lift is increased on the left wing, drag is also increased on that same wing. This causes the airplane to be pushed slightly to the left.

To overcome this, the pilot will push the right rudder pedal. So, in most cases, the pilot uses both the ailerons and the rudder to turn the aircraft.

Propulsion

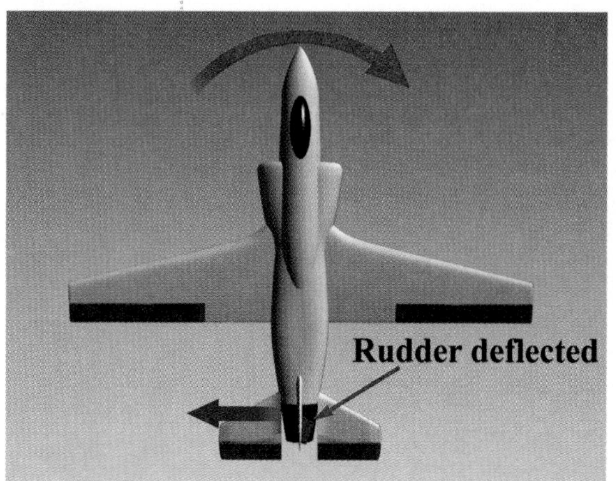

Propulsion is the science of designing an engine to propel or push a vehicle forward or up. For aviation there are two types of propulsion: air breathing and rocket propulsion. They both work on the principle of pushing high-speed exhaust gases out the back end, but they are different in one important way. An air-breathing engine uses the airstream it is in to help with propulsion, saving fuel. A rocket engine is made for traveling in space, where there is no air, so it must carry all of its fuel internally. An air-breathing engine will have an inlet and an outlet, while the rocket will be closed in the front and only have an exit. In general, an air-breathing engine will use less fuel than a rocket for the same amount of thrust.

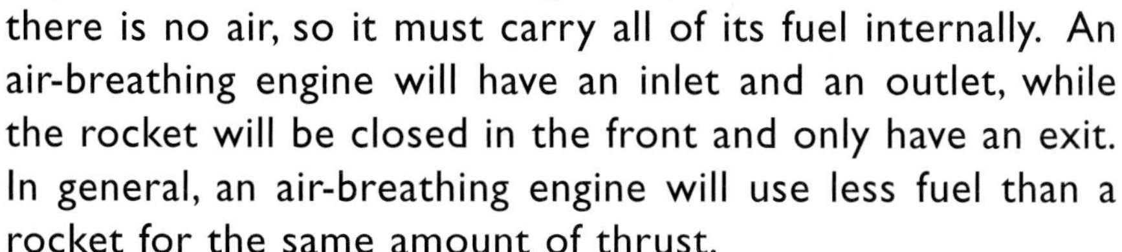

Thrust is generated by the engines of the airplane. The air flows into the engine at the same speed as the flight speed of the airplane, and exits the engine flowing much hotter and faster. The amount of thrust can be computed knowing how fast the air is moving as it enters and leaves the aircraft. The exhaust gases flow out the back of the engine, causing a reaction force on the airplane, pushing it forward. This concept is called the *reaction thrust principle*.

An easy way to demonstrate this principle is to take a balloon and blow it up, filling it with high-pressure air. Point the opening down and let go. As the high-pressure air inside the balloon escapes it pushes the balloon up.

History

The idea of using the reaction thrust principle for propulsion is not new. Hero of Alexandria designed a type of steam *turbine* called an aeolipile about 2000 years ago. The Chinese have used black-powder or gunpowder rockets since the twelfth century. Sir Isaac Newton described the reaction thrust principle in his laws of dynamics in 1687.

In 1791 John Barber of England was granted the first patent for a gas turbine, but it was almost 100 years before the necessary materials, designs, and manufacturing techniques made it possible to build one. Early air-breathing engines, like the Wright Flyer, used a small gas engine to power a large propeller to help speed up the air to generate thrust. Unfortunately, a propeller-driven engine is limited to slower speeds. In order to fly faster, to approach the speed of sound and beyond, another design or air-breathing engine was needed.

FUN FACTS

✔ The Wright brothers made it to the moon. Astronauts Armstrong and Aldrin carried a piece of the 1903 Wright Flyer to the moon on their trip in July 1969.

During the 1930s a German engineer, Hans von Ohain, and an English engineer, Frank Whittle, were each separately trying to design a new type of engine. By 1938 Hans von Ohain and his mechanic Max Hahn had designed, built, and test flown a jet aircraft. His design included a *compressor*, which is similar to a fan, and a turbine on the same shaft. Frank Whittle's design also included an internal fan or propeller run by a turbine with a *combustor*. His jet aircraft successfully flew in 1941. Thus, both England and Germany entered the jet aircraft age!

Since then, many improvements and variations of jet engine designs have been developed. In addition, lighter, more efficient jet engines made larger, faster airplanes possible. In under 100 years, airplanes have gone from the Wright Flyer and its first flight of 12 seconds and 120 feet to supersonic aircraft that fly all over the globe in 3 hours. All of this made possible with the invention of the air-breathing engine!

Components

The basic components of an air-breathing jet engine are the inlet, a compressor or fan, the combustor or burner, a turbine, and an exit *nozzle*. Different engines will use these components in various combinations. Some engine designs even leave out one or more of these components. But these are the basic building blocks of an engine.

Inlet

The design of the inlet, or air intake, helps determine the amount of air flow into an engine. After deciding the cruise speed of the aircraft, engineers design the inlet to suck in as much of the air coming toward it as needed. Subsonic, supersonic, and hypersonic cruise speeds each require a different inlet design. Inside the engine the next component, the compressor, works much better when the air enters fairly slowly, usually much slower than cruise velocity, so the inner walls of the inlet are designed to slow the velocity of the air stream as it comes to the compressor.

Compressor

The compressor is used to squeeze the air, or to increase the pressure of the air flow. This is vital to creating thrust. More pressure produces more thrust. To increase the pressure you must blow harder. The purpose of the compressor is to increase the pressure of the incoming air or power. Typical compressors increase the pressure of the air by 15 to 30 times the original pressure. Usually, an engine designer will choose among different compressors to find the compression ratio that fits the specifications of the airplane being built.

Combustor

The slow-moving, high-pressure air from the compressor is fed into the combustor or burner where it is mixed with a highly flammable fuel and ignited. The very hot, high-pressure air leaving the burner will be used to generate the thrust. These gases are very, very hot, and the engineer must carefully design heat-resistant components that come after the burner that won't melt or deform.

The combustion engineer works with the mixture of fuel and air to get just the right combination for a good, hot burn. Too little fuel and the mixture won't burn hot enough to produce the needed thrust. Too much fuel and the mixture won't burn, completely wasting valuable fuel. Sometimes a second burner is used after the turbine. The second burner reheats gases just before they escape, to increase velocity and generate more thrust.

Turbine

The high-temperature, high-pressure gases are released from the burner and passed into the turbine or engine where the local pressures are much lower. The high-pressure gases begin to drop in pressure. As the pressure drops, the velocity of the flow of exhaust gases increases. As these gases leave the engine they generate thrust. Part of this flow may also be used to power the compressor. Although this decreases overall thrust, it is more efficient than having a separate power source for the compressor.

An engineer must be very careful in the design of a turbine because of the high temperature of gases coming from the burner. If the materials in the turbine blades are not chosen well, the blades can melt, deform, and be less efficient, or even break off and destroy the rest of the turbine.

Nozzle

The inside walls of the exit nozzle are shaped so that the exhaust gases continue to increase their velocity as they travel out of the engine. The higher the exit velocity of the gases, the more thrust can be generated. Some fighter aircraft have adjustable nozzles, allowing the pilot to adjust thrust as needed. Other nozzles are of a fixed design because conditions do not change enough to need adjustability. Again, the engineer must be concerned with the temperatures of the exhaust gases in the exit nozzle, especially if there is an *afterburner*. If the walls on the inside of the nozzle melt and change, then the exhaust velocities and thrust may not be correct.

FUN FACTS

✔ In China, bats are believed to be nature's helpers and friends of the earth. The Chinese Wu-fu symbol (five bats circling the Tree of Life) has long been considered a good luck symbol.

Types of Air-Breathing Engines

There are four basic types of air-breathing engines: the *turbojet*, the *turboprop*, the *turbofan*, and the *ramjet*. Each has its advantages and disadvantages for specific cruise speeds. Engineers look for two things when designing a jet engine: thrust-to-weight ratio and fuel consumption. Most aircraft are designed for low fuel consumption, even though it means lower thrust capability. Some aircraft, such as fighter jets, need a lot of thrust and are not as concerned about the amount of fuel used, if the mission requires it. Engineers recommend which engines work best in different conditions.

Turbojet

The original jet engine, discussed in the History section, became known as the turbojet. This engine completely changed air transportation. It greatly reduced the expense of air travel and improved aircraft safety. The turbojet also allowed faster speeds, even supersonic speeds. It had a much higher thrust-per-unit weight ratio than the piston-driven engines, which led directly to longer flight distances and higher payloads, meaning more passengers and baggage. As it happened, it also has lower maintenance costs.

The typical turbojet engine has all five of the components described in the previous section: an inlet, a compressor, a combustor, a turbine, and a nozzle. The figure at right shows a basic turbojet schematic with the five components clearly identified.

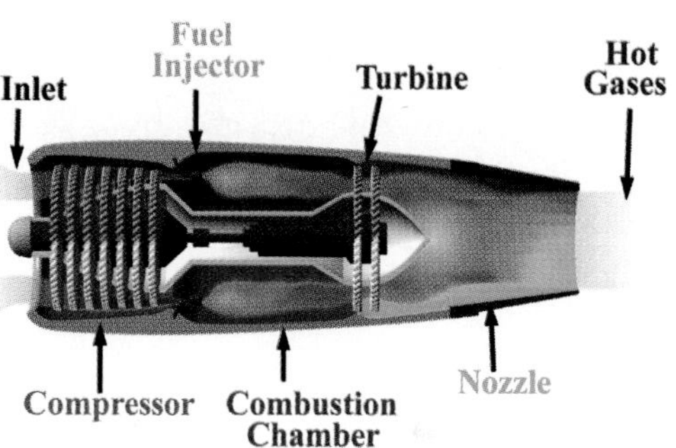

Turbojet engine.

To get an increased thrust, an afterburner can be added to the turbojet. Most aircraft do not use an afterburner because they use so much fuel. Fighter aircraft with afterburners only use them when absolutely necessary. If a pilot runs too long with the afterburner on, he or she risks running low on fuel before the mission is completed.

Remember from the components section, that temperature is a very important factor when designing the turbine. The exhaust cannot be too hot or it will melt parts (such as the blades) in the turbine. However, the hotter the exhaust the more thrust there will be. The engineers use a technique called "turbine blade cooling." This allows hotter than normal exhaust from the combustor to enter the turbine engine. Cool air from the compressor is fed into hollow turbine blades, so they won't become overheated and warp or break. The cooling must be controlled very carefully to get maximum thrust.

The turbojet engine is the most popular engine for most high-speed aircraft, in spite of the higher fuel consumption. When high speed and performance are important, the cost of fuel is less important. Military fighters and fast business jets use turbojet engines.

Turboprop

Soon after the first turbojets were in the air, the turboprop engine was developed. The advantage of turboprops is fuel efficiency at lower speeds. This engine design produces two thrusts, one with the propeller and the other through exhaust. A large gear box makes it possible for the turbine to turn a large propeller at high speed, producing the first thrust.

As the propeller speed increases, the tips of the blades may approach supersonic speeds. If this happens, the flow may separate and shocks may form, decreasing the air flow into the engine. For these reasons the turboprop is restricted to slower speeds because of the large propeller. The majority of commuter aircraft are still driven by turboprops.

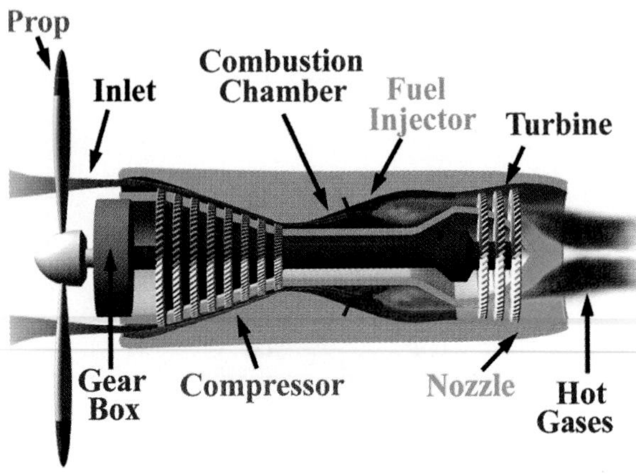

Turboprop engine.

The figure at left shows the basic components of a turboprop engine. The propeller precedes the inlet and the compressor, but it serves the same purpose. It provides a large volume of high-pressure air to the engine exhaust streams. An inlet and a compressor are used to send a part of the air flow to the burner. A turbine is used to power the propeller and the compressor, and the hot exhaust gases are accelerated out through the nozzle. (This is the second thrust, after the propeller.) Because only a small part of the air flow is actually burned inside the engine, the turboprop engine can generate a lot of thrust with a low fuel consumption compared to a turbojet engine. The turboprop is usually chosen for airplanes flying at lower speeds.

Turbofan

As engineers struggled to overcome the limitations of the turboprop engine for airplanes at higher speeds, a new design emerged: the turbofan—a compromise between the turboprop and the turbojet engines. The turbofan engine contains a large internal propeller, sometimes called a ducted fan, and two streams of air flow through it. The primary stream travels through all of the components like a turbojet engine, while the secondary stream is usually accelerated through a nozzle to mix with the primary exhaust stream. The figure at the top of the next page illustrates the design of a turbofan engine.

There are several advantages to the turbofan over the other two engines. The fan is not as large as a propeller and does not disrupt the airflow at higher velocities like the turboprop could. Also, by enclosing the fan inside a duct or cowling, the aerodynamics are better controlled. There is less flow separation at high speeds and less trouble with shocks developing.

A turbofan engine can fly at transonic speeds up to Mach 0.9. While the fan is smaller than the propeller, it sucks in more air flow than the turbojet engine, and so gets more thrust. Like the turboprop engine, the turbofan consumes less fuel than the turbojet. The turbofan is the engine of choice for high-speed, subsonic commercial airplanes.

While it is possible to put afterburners into one or both streams, the slight additional thrust gained is at the expense of a large increase in fuel consumption. Many newer fighters, like the F-16, use turbofans with afterburners.

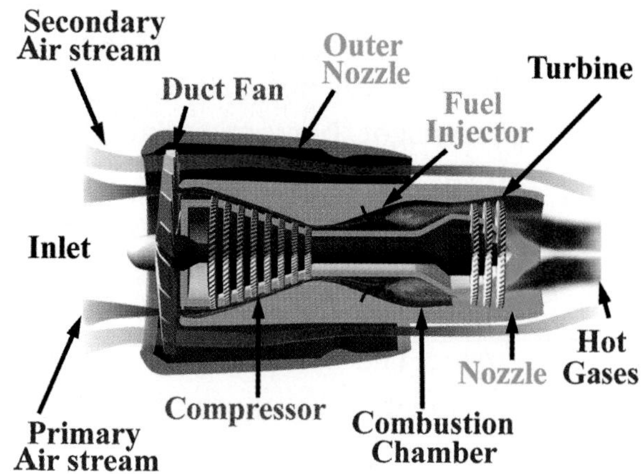

Turbofan engine.

Ramjets

Below Mach 1.0, a compressor is very much needed as a component of an air-breathing engine. As an airplane increases its speed past Mach 1.0, the air pressure created from the speed of the air flow decreases the need for a compressor. As speeds approach Mach 3.5-4.0, a compressor isn't even needed. At these speeds the ramjet is the most efficient engine because it has fewer components. The ramjet has no compressor or turbine, but has a much higher tolerance to high temperatures. It has an inlet, a burner, and a nozzle.

The limitations of a ramjet are that it will not work at less than supersonic speeds and that another engine must first power the aircraft to supersonic speeds and the fuel and air mixture must burn in the combustor. The ramjet inlet must slow the air flow from the supersonic speeds to subsonic speed for fuel ignition in the burner. As the ramjet approaches Mach 6.0 the air coming into the burner is too hot to burn! This is caused by the friction as the supersonic air is slowed at the inlet to subsonic speed. At this speed not enough thrust is being generated to continue performance.

There is a proposed solution to the ramjet's speed limitation (Mach 6.0). It is called supersonic combustion ramjet *(SCRAMJET)*. Instead of slowing the air flow down to subsonic speeds for combustion, the SCRAMJET will ignite the air while still supersonic, thus avoiding the friction at the inlet. Fuel must still be injected into the airstream to be ignited. Unfortunately, today's fuels do not ignite quickly enough. The development of a workable fuel injection system for the SCRAMJET is still in its early stages.

FUN FACTS

✔ The first astronaut to go into space as a scientist was Dr. Harrison Schmitt, a geologist, on Apollo 17. It was the last lunar mission.

Future of Propulsion

There is continuing research in the design of more efficient engines that use less fuel and generate higher thrust per weight. New material designs allow higher inlet temperatures. Improvements of the inlets, compressors, turbines, and nozzles are ongoing. A relatively new area, active control theory, is showing promising results. In an active control system, computer chips monitor the conditions throughout the engine. The computer may change the fuel and air ratio in the combustor slightly for a better burn, or it might change the shape of either the inlet or the exit nozzle slightly to improve the aerodynamics.

Supersonic and hypersonic engine design is particularly challenging. Today's airplanes, especially military aircraft, must fly in many different conditions: subsonic, supersonic and hypersonic. Hybrid or mixed combinations of the turbojet, ramjet, and rocket engines are the focus of study these days. Several are in their design stages now.

Parts in a Spacecraft

Spacecraft have different requirements and missions. Spacecraft spend most of their existence in space where there is no atmosphere. Even though the space shuttle has wings, it does not use those wings to fly in space.

Why not? Let's look at each phase of the space shuttle's flight. First there is takeoff. The shuttle does not fly into space on its own. It is carried into space by rockets. The shuttle is "the payload" that is launched into space.

Once the shuttle is in space it doesn't really use its wings. Recall our discussion of Bernoulli's Theorem and Newton's Laws. In both cases we talked about air flow. But there is no air in space!

The wings on the space shuttle are used to re-enter the earth's atmosphere and land. It is a glider and does not have an engine that is used for landing!

Spacecraft have unique requirements and are very expensive to build, maintain, and use. It costs millions of dollars to send the shuttle into space. Engineers and scientists develop ways to make sure that only the essentials are carried on board. Even a few extra pounds cost a great deal of money.

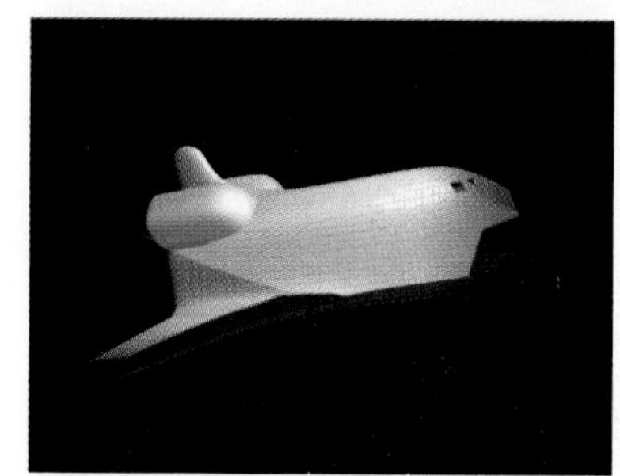

Unlike an airplane that makes short trips, the shuttle's missions last about a week. What would you bring with you if you were going on a trip for a week? There's no place to shop for goods you might need. Think of it as a hiking trip in the wilderness. You won't want to bring unnecessary things (you would have to carry them). What would you bring?

Food and water are essentials! But believe it or not the shuttle does not bring drinking water for the astronauts. It makes its own water, which is one of the by-products of its energy systems.

If you were driving instead of hiking and there was no place to stop for gas along the way, what would you do? You would bring additional fuel. Air-breathing engines used by cars, planes, and most other land vehicles carry their own propellent and use the oxygen in the air around the engine as the oxidizer. What happens in space where there is no oxygen to combust the fuel? You would need to bring it with you.

You might also consider other types of energy such as batteries or solar power. Many satellites have solar panels and cells that use the energy from the sun and convert it into power.

Spacecraft have shells that must withstand severe temperatures. During re-entry, the heat on the outside of the vehicle can become so hot that it chars the surface and actually chemically reacts with other air particles. For this reason, scientists and engineers are always looking for new and improved materials.

Whether the goal is to improve existing engines for the world's transportation needs, or designing the engines for future supersonic and hypersonic aircraft, there is always demand for more engineers and more ideas.

FUN FACTS

✔ The original names for the space shuttles were the Constitution, Discover Challenger, and Atlantis. The Constitution was renamed the Enterprise.

Paper Tail

15 minutes

MATERIALS

- 2 sheets of colored construction paper
- safety scissors
- clear plastic tape
- 16 – 20 inches of string or ribbon

STEPS TO FOLLOW:

1. **Cut a 2-inch by 11-inch wide strip from the paper.**
2. **Attach the string to one end of the strip with a piece of tape.**
3. **Hold the end of the string and whip the paper back and forth in front of you. Observe the tail.**
4. **Cut a 1/4-inch by 12-inch strip from the paper.**
5. **Attach the thin strip of paper to the wide strip.**
6. **Again whip the strip back and forth in front of you. Observe what happens this time. How does it move now? Is it the same or different?**

SCIENCE EXPLANATION:

Why do we put tails on kites? Tails provide stability to flying objects. As you move a wide strip of paper back and forth you see erratic movements. When you make a tail you observe that the paper moves smoothly through the air. This demonstrates the effect of a kite's tail as it flies. It also demonstrates how a bird's tail feather works to create a smoother air flow as birds navigate through turbulent air flows or warm thermals.

Structures

STEPS TO FOLLOW:

1 **First, using only the marshmallows and spaghetti, construct a tower that will support a box of paper clips.**

2 **Next, a greater challenge. You must construct a bridge using only the listed materials to support the 2 liter bottle.**

3 **The bridge needs to be long enough to span the distance (use books, desks, or tables to create the space to be spanned) and strong enough to hold the weight of the liter bottle.**

4 **If possible, have your friends make their own bridge. Have a contest and see whose bridge holds the most weight. Also consider the cost of construction by placing a dollar value on each piece: $100 for each marshmallow, $50 for each piece of spaghetti. Try to get the strongest structure for the least amount of money.**

MATERIALS

- 10 oz. bag of miniature marshmallows
- 1 lb box of spaghetti (uncooked)
- 1 box of paper clips
- ruler or tape measure
- pad of notebook paper for drawing designs
- pencil
- straight drinking straws
- box of toothpicks
- clear plastic tape
- safety scissors
- 2 liter bottle filled with water (about 5 lbs.) for testing the bridge

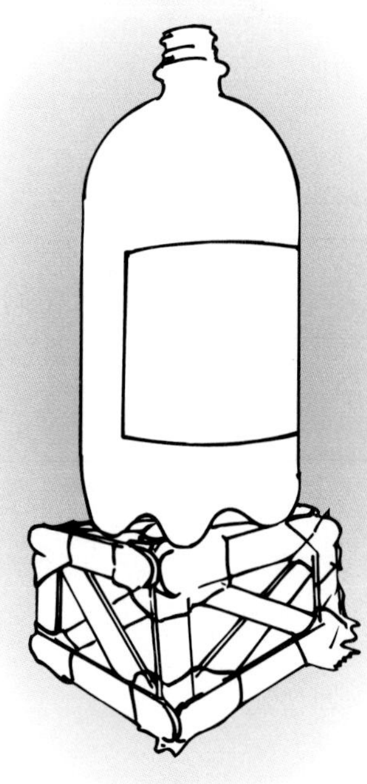

SCIENCE EXPLANATION:

Structures is a very important field in aeronautical and aerospace engineering. Vehicles must be strong but lightweight. On earth the designers of buildings and other structures do not have to be as concerned about weight. Using beams, spars, and trusses makes a structure stronger. A truss construction made with these materials will yield a structure strong enough to support the weight. Once you overcome that obstacle, it is more of a challenge to figure out how to do it inexpensively.

Controls

MATERIALS

- clay
- 3 wooden skewers (approximately 8 inches long)
- clear plastic tape
- safety scissors
- aluminum foil
- sponge

STEPS TO FOLLOW:

1 **Make a small clay model of an airplane. Using the aluminum foil, wrap the different parts of the airplane so that it is completely covered.**

2 **Push a wooden skewer through your model from the nose to the tail of the airplane (the longitudinal axis). Make sure that part of the skewer sticks out of either side of your airplane.**

3 **Push another skewer through one wing through the fuselage and out the other side through the fuselage (on the lateral axis). Make sure that part of the skewer sticks out of either side of your airplane. If the sticks are too long, cut them with the scissors.**

4 **At the point where the two skewers appear to intersect, push another skewer through the top of the fuselage and out the bottom. Make sure that part of the skewer sticks out of either side of your airplane. If the sticks are too long, cut them with the scissors. Use the sponge as a platform for your airplane. The skewer coming out the bottom of the plane can be inserted into the sponge.**

5 **Slowly twirl your plane holding either end of a stick. Are you demonstrating pitch, roll or yaw? Try this with all the different sticks in your airplane. What part of your airplane moves when you twirl the stick?**

SCIENCE EXPLANATION:

The control surfaces, the ailerons, the elevators, and the rudder, on any flying vehicle are used to change the forces on the vehicle. They are also used to allow the pilot to move the vehicle in the direction he or she wants. An airplane can basically move in six different ways; these are called the six degrees of freedom of motion.

Ailerons located on the wings control banking or roll to the right or left around the longitudinal axis. The elevators are the horizontal flaps on the tail assembly. Elevators control the climbing or diving motion (pitch) around the lateral axis. The rudder is the vertical flap on the tail assembly. It controls the turning or yaw motion around the vertical axis.

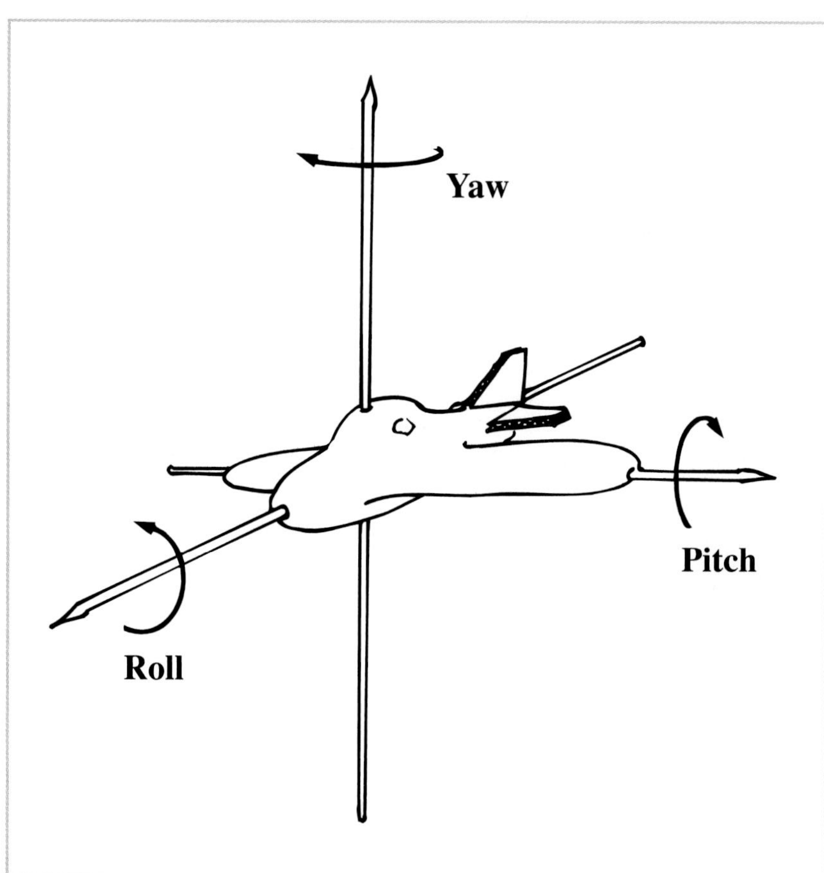

Rocket Balloon

20 minutes

MATERIALS

- long balloon
- straight drinking straw
- 12 feet of string or fishing line
- clear plastic tape
- two chairs, any height

STEPS TO FOLLOW:

1 **Thread the string through the straw.**

2 **Tie the string between two chairs approximately 12 feet apart.**

3 **Blow up the balloon.**

4 **While holding the balloon shut with one hand, secure the balloon with tape to the straw length-wise as shown below.**

5 **Release the balloon from one end of the string. Observe what happens. (The balloon and straw are propelled to the end of the string.)**

SCIENCE EXPLANATION:

Newton's Third Law of Motion states that for every action there is an opposite and equal reaction. The balloon and straw shot up the line when you let go. In this case, the air escaping out the back of the balloon is the action. The opposite reaction propels the balloon forward along the string.

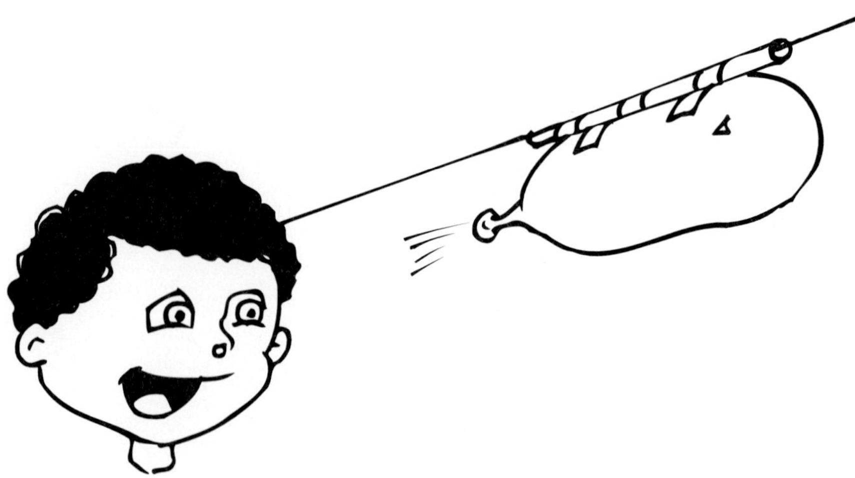

Stability

STEPS TO FOLLOW:

1 Take a ruler and hairbrush and place a coin on one end of the ruler. (The hairbrush is used under the ruler in the center point to create a seesaw.)

2 Remove the coin. What happens?

3 Place the seesaw on a stack of books, so that the seesaw swings up and down.

4 Repeat the experiment. This time record how long it takes for the ruler to return to its original position.

5 minutes

MATERIALS

- ruler
- erasers, coins, or small rocks
- hairbrush
- a 2-inch-thick book, any length
- watch

SCIENCE EXPLANATION:

Stability for an airplane means that it will resist change in direction and even restore itself to the original course. Stability can either be static or dynamic. Static stability means that when you move an object it returns to its original position. Dynamic stability is concerned with how much time it may take for the object to return to its original position.

Inside the Space Station

60 minutes

MATERIALS

- glue
- safety scissors
- plastic containers and tops that can be thrown away
- 2 sheets of colored construction paper
- plastic strawberry basket
- egg carton
- aluminum foil
- velcro
- empty toilet paper tubes
- shoe box
- clear plastic tape
- clay
- action or small soldier figures
- felt squares
- a roll of clear fishing line

STEPS TO FOLLOW:

1 **Using the materials listed or others that you can think of, construct a model of one of the space stations. Use your imagination. You might be able to improve on the design of the next space station!**

2 **To build the model of the inside of the space station, use one of the empty boxes. Plan out the space. There will need to be a place for the crew to work and live. Remember, since there's no gravity in space there is no such thing as "up" or "down" on a spacecraft. Don't forget that things in space float if they aren't secured; use the velcro to secure items inside your space station. Use the clear fishing line to hang things in your station to simulate floating in space.**

SCIENCE EVALUATION:

Living and working in space for long periods of time is one of NASA's great challenges. The hostile environment of space and low gravity conditions have resulted in new ways of thinking about how men and women will survive. Like the early pioneers that crossed the plains, you must bring everything you need

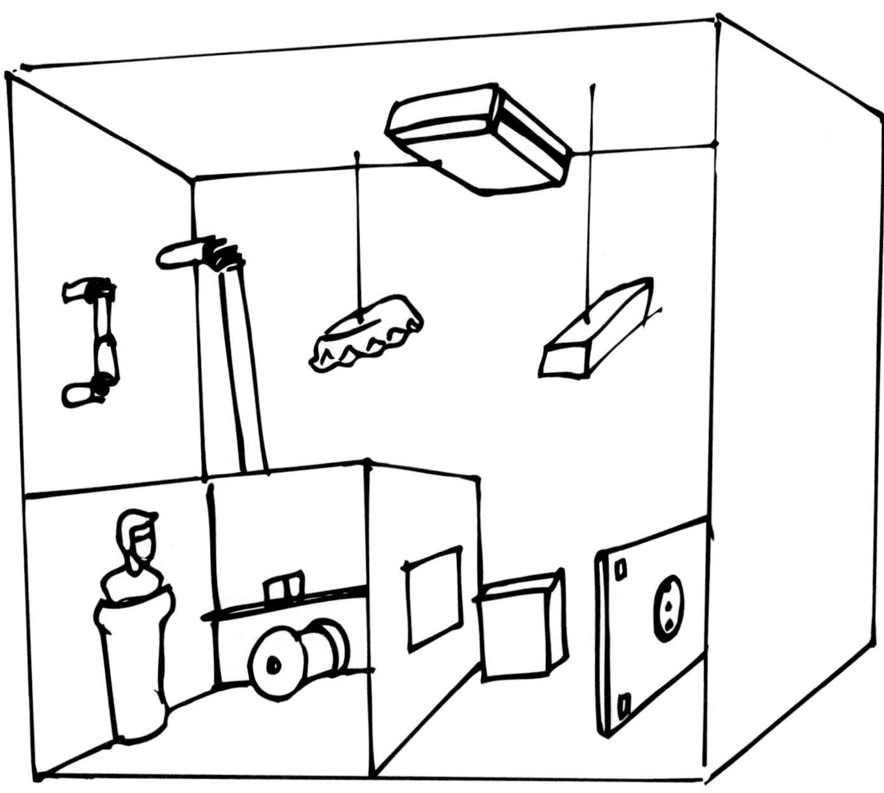

with you; there's no store around the corner. At the same time, bringing everything is not possible due to the expense.

The space stations provide a place to live and study the long, term effects of space on humans as well as a place to work and conduct scientific research. Objects have to be secured, otherwise they will float around. Also, there's no wasted space. You can use the "ceiling" of a space vehicle as well as its floor.

CHAPTER 5

Man-Made Flyers

The principles of flight are used over and over again on a vast variety of shapes and sizes of man-made flying machines. From the most simple and ancient of instruments to today's high-tech, state-of-the-art experimental aircraft, each object must obey the same physical laws which govern flight.

Kites

Where did kites originate? Some think they came from China or the Middle East. Others believe they came from the South Pacific Islands. Even the Balinese have their own story! Nevertheless, we are left with a heritage of wonderful stories, designs, and techniques for flying kites.

Kites have been used for a variety of purposes in different cultures throughout the world. Some cultures used kites to communicate with spirits. Other cultures used kites for practical purposes. In the Solomon Islands they are used in lieu of a fishing rod. In Korea they are used to announce the birth of a child. In China they were used during battles—the bamboo they were made of hummed and shrieked in the wind, frightening the enemy. In both China and Japan kites were capable of holding or "flying" a person in the air to spy or act as a sniper using bows and arrows. In India and Japan some of the best "fighter" kites were developed. Fighter kites are a specialty that can be enjoyed at some kite festivals.

FUN FACTS

✔ The Fisherman bat is one of two or three kinds of bats in the world that eat fish. These bats have long legs and claws, and using echolocation to find their way, they are able to swoop to the water and scoop up a fish. Their fur sheds water, and they can swim.

There is good luck associated with kites. In some cultures, when the line of the kite is cut, the kite takes away the bad luck or the evil spirits. In Thailand the kites are used to communicate with the gods so that monsoons will not be so bad and the crops will be saved from the floods.

How did kites reach Europe? There are many theories. Some believe that European travelers brought the idea back from China. Certainly the cultures in the Middle East had been using kites for centuries. In Rome, windsock banners that looked like dragons were used for military and religious purposes. For a short time, Europeans used kites during hunting to flush out birds from the bushes. The kites would get stuck in the bushes, so the hunters found other ways to find the birds.

Later kites were used for scientific purposes! Benjamin Franklin, who had flown kites for fun, used a kite in 1752 to find out if there was an electrical charge in clouds. In 1750 Dr. Alexander Wilson of Edinburgh put a thermometer on a kite and sent the kite up to test air temperatures at different altitudes. Later, wind speeds at different altitudes were measured. We do the same thing today using weather balloons!

FUN FACTS

✔ Many experimental aircraft are first flown remotely by test pilots. These aircraft are generally smaller versions of proposed aircraft. The pilots sit in a cockpit on the ground and maneuver the vehicle in the air. This allows the test pilot to check out new vehicles in a safe environment.

Dr. Alexander Graham Bell, Otto Lilienthal, Octave Chanute, and the Wright Brothers all studied kites to learn more about flight. Dr. Alexander Bell, who invented the telephone, used kites to learn more about weather. He also contributed to aviation by experimenting with kites to learn more about the possibility of enabling people to fly. Like the Chinese and the Japanese, he developed a kite that could raise a person up in the air. He developed what is called the tetrahedral cell. It had great strength and a light structure.

Samuel Cody (Buffalo Bill) used kites in his famous "Wild West Shows" in England. He and his son Leon developed larger and larger kites and competed against each other by using them to tow boats across the English Channel! They later helped the French and Russians develop observation kite systems for war time. These same designs are used today for kite festivals and competitions.

How Do Kites Fly?

Let's explore the aerodynamics of kites. Kites are heavier-than-air devices. They weigh more than the volume of air they displace. They are flown at the end of a string, line, or rope. Kites are aerodynes—they overcome the force of gravity and are kept in the air by lift, the force of the wind, or wind pressure on them. Lift is exerted in an upward direction, thereby opposing the pull of gravity on the kite.

There are two principles involved in the aerodynamics of kite flight. One is Newton's Third Law, which states that for every action there is an equal and opposite reaction. Think of the kite as flying on an inclined plane and flying in one spot. The kite exerts a downward force upon the air. The air passes over the top edge of the kite and goes down the upper surface of the kite. Remember that air is relatively heavy. As the kite pushes downward, it gets an equal push upward by the air. As this happens, the kite gets an upward counter force and it flies! Second, the lower pressure above the kite's upper surface allows the kite to lift.

FUN FACTS

✔ NASA does not allow married couples to fly together in space. The exception to the rule occurred in 1992. Dr. Jan Davis and her husband Mark Lee, who had trained together, decided to get married before their space shuttle mission. NASA allowed them to fly together as a "wedding present."

Knowing these basic principles can help us learn how to design and fly a kite. Also, knowing the strength and direction of the wind can help us to develop a knowledge of the basic moves and tricks in kite flying.

Successfully flying a kite involves the proper *angle of attack* or *flying angle* in relation to the wind. The angle of attack is the angle by which the kite is inclined in relation to the direction of the air moving toward it. This angle can be altered both by the design and by the position of the kite to the wind, such as by string or cord control.

The flying angle of a kite can also be changed by making adjustments to lines attached to the kite, such as the "*bridle*" or the tail. Each adjustment adds or subtracts to the ability of the kite to maintain angle of attack, balance, and stability. A kite does not have perfect balance and stability. It pitches forward, backward, and side to side. It stalls and dives. All these qualities make kites both a thrill and a challenge to fly successfully.

The tail of a kite adds to its stability and balance, limiting the maximum altitude that can be reached. One must consider the pros and cons to each element of kite design. For example, one can eliminate the tail, but bow out or curve the design for stability and greater altitude. Similarly, one can change the cover material or frame, add wings or keels, or use different shaped wing surfaces. Rudders and tapering are some other design possibilities. To build your own kite, look at the Kite Flying activity at the end of this chapter.

Once you've become more skilled with kites, investigate stunt or novelty kites. Kites can also carry balloons, banners, and other decorations. Attach a camera to a kite and with a timed shutter release, take a picture. Fly kites in tandem (hooked to each other), or like the people of the Solomon Islands, try fishing with a kite. The possibilities are endless.

Visit the kite festivals in your area. Join a kite club or start one in your school or community. Look up kite societies and associations on the Internet. You can learn everything from kite safety and the basics for beginner hobbyists, to first aid for your kite and more technical skills for flying fighter and stunt kites.

Like the great inventors, keep working and experimenting until your kite flies. Learning from failure is the essence of invention and progress. Now, go fly a kite!

Parachutes

Throughout time many have tried to fly by jumping off something, hoping to land safely. Most jumps failed, but a few successes gave people the false hope that humans could fly alone.

In the chapter on *The History of Air and Space Flight* it was discussed that the first recorded parachute jump took place in 852 A.D. when Arman Firman tried to fly in Cordoba, Spain. He jumped off of a tower wearing a huge cloak. He thought the cloak would billow out and allow him to float gently to the earth. Instead, the cloak did nothing to slow him down and he crashed to the ground.

FUN FACTS

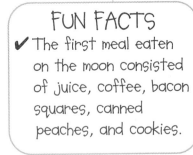

✔ The first meal eaten on the moon consisted of juice, coffee, bacon squares, canned peaches, and cookies.

Although Firman may have been the first to jump, many experts credit Leonardo da Vinci (the famous painter and inventor) for the earliest studies on flight. Among his first drawings about flight was the parachute. He wrote, "If a man has a tent of closely woven linen without any apertures or openings, 12 braccia across and 12 in depth, he can throw himself down from any great height without injury." He studied flight for over 20 years, and from 1486 to his death in 1519 studied birds, convinced that the secret to human flight could be found in their wings.

It was not until 1909, when the Wright brothers developed powered flight, that the parachute found a new purpose. In 1912 Capt. Albert Berry of the United States Army made the first successful descent by parachute from an airplane. Early parachutes were made of canvas, and later of silk. In World War I, parachutes were used by observers to escape from damaged observation balloons but were considered impractical for airplanes. In the last stages of World War I new parachute designs made jumping from an airplane possible. Because of this success the U.S. Government formed a special "parachute" board to design parachutes for various uses in an aircraft. As a result, by World War II parachutes were used for many different purposes.

FUN FACTS

✔ More bats are found in the tropics than any other mammal.

During World War II thousands of soldiers parachuted from airplanes. After the war many of these veterans continued to parachute for fun. In 1951 the first world parachuting championship was held in Yugoslavia. In 1960 there were approximately 1000 who participated in the sport. In 1980, just 20 years later, the sport had grown to some 250,000 individuals participating in 28 different countries.

Today parachutes are used for dropping food and medical supplies into areas stricken by disasters like floods and earthquakes. Life rafts and other survival equipment are lowered by parachute in air-sea rescue operations. Equipment weighing many tons can be dropped from an aircraft by parachute. Parachutes also serve as landing breaks for high-speed jet airplanes and have been used to slow returning space capsules.

Why do we need a parachute? Objects falling freely through the atmosphere are pulled toward the earth by gravity. Free-falling objects can attain great speed! Skydivers fall at speeds of 110-130 MPH during formation jumps and near 200 MPH during other types of maneuvers. By using a parachute, the speed of fall is reduced enough to insure a safe landing. The open parachute counters the downward pull of gravity.

Today parachutes are made of nylon. The major components of a parachute system include the main parachute, harness and container system, and the reserve parachute. Sport parachutists carry both a main and reserve parachute attached to a single harness system.

There are various ways to deploy a parachute. The parachutist may pull a rip cord with his or her hand. A static line connected to the aircraft can deploy the parachute as the person jumps. Some military aircraft have ejection seat systems which contain parachutes. Generally these systems can be activated automatically or manually. Today, most sport parachutes are rectangular ram-air types. These parachutes are composed of top and bottom surface panels with dividers that create "cells." There are typically 5 to 9 cells in a modern parachute, although some parachutes may have up to 27 cells! Compared to the older round canopy parachutes, ram-air parachutes have superior aerodynamics and the forward horizontal and vertical speeds can be controlled by the parachutist.

FUN FACT:

✔ The first man and woman in space were Yuri Gagarin and Valentina Tereshkova of the Soviet Union.

To find out more about parachuting: check out some library books on parachuting, sky-diving, or air sports or write a local parachuting company for information.

Gliders

Although there have been many myths and legends about people trying to fly or glide, the first person to write about the principle of "lift" was Sir George Cayley. By 1799, Cayley had made the single most important discovery in the history of aviation. He found that air flowing over the top of a curved, fixed wing will create "lift," an upward force that can cause the wing to rise.

Cayley also found that the larger the wing, and the faster the flow of air over it, the greater the lift created. He also discovered that some sort of tail was needed for stability.

As discussed in the chapter *The History of Air and Space Flight*, the next person to advance the knowledge of flight was Otto Lilienthal, who designed and constructed hang gliders. Warm air rising up the hill helped "lift" the glider, which would skim a few feet above the ground for 150 feet or more. He made over 2000 flights in his hang gliders.

With each flight Lilienthal learned a little more about how to control a glider in each of the three dimensions of flight: roll—tipping from side to side; pitch—the nose moving up and down; and yaw—turning right to left. Methodically, he developed gliders that were more easily controlled and could be flown more steadily and in stronger winds.

There was one problem, though. All of his flights ended with the glider diving headlong into the ground. Adding a tail with a vertical structure helped keep the glider stable and added distance, but the end of the flight was still the same—the glider would pitch forward and down. He gradually realized it was the angle of the wing to the wind that caused the problem. Today this problem is called a "stall."

Normally, the air flows across the wing toward the trailing edge, causing lift. A stall is the result of the air flow separating as it flows across the top of the wing. The air "burbles" off into space and the wing loses its lifting power.

Now, if the wing is angled up too steeply, the air stream is interrupted and lifting power is lost, creating a stall. The pilot may feel a shudder or quiver, then pitch downward. If the vehicle is not high enough to recover it will dive into the ground. It was due to a stall that Lilienthal fell to his death in 1896.

Today, because gliders can be towed to 5000 or more feet, they generally have sufficient height to pull out of a stall. Gliders also have instruments and control surfaces to change the angle of the wing to pull out of a stall.

What began as a curiosity has now become a very popular sport. Glider events are now worldwide. First came the Otto Lilienthal Meet, an informal gathering of visionary self-launched flying enthusiasts. Then came a few regional contests and then national and world meets. Competitions between individuals, teams, clubs, and nations are now held every year.

FUN FACTS

✔ The astronauts' nickname for their adjustable seats in the early space capsules was the "barber chair."

Blimps

The history of blimps dates back to the year 1783. It was in this year when the Montgolfier brothers of Annonay, France, sent the first hot-air balloon aloft. Ever since that first balloon, inventors have been trying to design better airships, or dirigibles—blimps.

The earliest blimp designs consisted of taking a round balloon and stretching it at both ends to form an egg shape. These early blimps maintained their shape by internal gas pressure.

These nonrigid blimp designs would often buckle under the strain of heavy loads or rough weather.

This problem was overcome by giving later blimps a semi-rigid design by adding a light-weight *keel,* or a rigid frame, along the bottom of the blimp. The keel took some of the stress off of the blimp *envelope*, or skin, and made larger blimps possible.

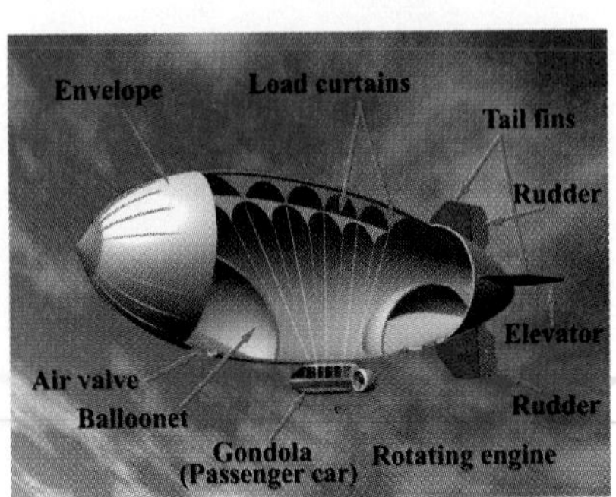

The parts of a blimp.

The next major improvements in blimp design came many years later. Count Ferdinand von Zeppelin envisioned a semi-rigid dirigible, or airship, evolving into one that was rigid. The new design held the envelope rigid by a metal skeleton attached to a much bigger, stronger keel. This rigid design freed the blimp's envelope from needing internal pressure to maintain its shape. This design, which is used in the present day, allowed Zeppelin to use self-contained cells, filled with gas and wired into place, instead of one large envelope.

Blimps have four main components: the envelope, the *gondola*, the *power plant,* and the controls.

A blimp's envelope is the "skin" that holds the ship's contents together. Early envelopes consisted of various cloths, fabrics, or silks stretched into the familiar oval blimp shape. These early envelope designs often tore or caught fire. Today, modern materials make an envelope of greater strength and lighter weight possible. For example, the French firm Aerazure builds blimp envelopes by taking two layers of a synthetic, a man-made material, and soaking them with titanium dioxide. A thin, strong, gas-tight membrane is then sandwiched between them. Panels of this material are then stitched together to create the blimp's envelope.

The next part of a blimp is a gondola, a box or cabin that is attached underneath the blimp. The early, nonrigid blimps could only carry a small gondola that held a few people. Later, by the 1930s, when the blimps had a rigid frame, bigger gondolas could comfortably hold more than 100 passengers. Blimps of this era carried gondolas containing passenger cabins, a promenade for viewing the land below, dining rooms, reading and writing rooms, complete kitchens, and even the first showers on board an airship. Today's typical blimps are rarely used for commercial use and only carry seven or eight passengers plus two pilots.

In 1852 Henri Giffard installed a small steam engine in the gondola of a spindle-shaped balloon. This engine turned a propeller that pulled the airship through the air at a speed of 5 miles per hour against the wind. But steam engines were too big and dangerous to use. Later, in 1898, Alberto Santos-Dumont began to experiment with gasoline engines as a power source for balloons. On October 19, 1901, he steered his cigar-shaped balloon over a 7-mile course above Paris, France, for which Santos-Dumont received much acclaim.

Today's engines have improved upon Santos-Dumont's design immensely. For example, the Airship Industries Sky Ship 500 HL uses two Porsche 930 engines to push 15,000 pounds of blimp through the air at speeds up to 45 knots (about 83 MPH). Each engine is contained within the gondola in a fireproof box. The engines can turn a tail rotor, propeller, or the two main five-blade variable pitch propellers. This propeller assembly rotates inside a duct, called a vector, and provides quiet, efficient thrust. Thus, the pilot may turn the propellers in the direction he or she wishes to go—up, down, or forward.

FUN FACTS

✔ "Orbital velocity" refers to the speed needed to keep an object in orbit. The orbital velocity for the Earth is 18,000 miles per hour.

The controls of a blimp have also seen much advancement from the early days of blimp design. Early balloons could be steered as they went up and down, but once aloft the prevailing wind would take over. Several methods of steering were tried, but none of them were successful. It was Alberto Santos-Dumont, again, who gained credit for building the first dirigible that could be maneuvered forward through the air. He did this by using propellers. Soon blimps were propelled by engines and propellers and maneuvered by rudders for forward movement and by elevators for up-and-down movement. Today's blimps are controlled in much the same way.

Blimps are commonly seen at sporting events.

In the early 1900s there was great interest in the military use of blimps. Germany took the lead in blimp design through Count Ferdinand von Zeppelin, and during World War I used von Zeppelin's rigid blimp design to bomb London. However, the cumbersome blimps proved to be easy targets for the defending British airplanes.

Early in the 1900s von Zeppelin and Alfred Colsman foresaw that blimps could be used for transportation of passengers as well as for military uses. They formed the German Airship Transport Company in 1909, which is still in existence today.

Soon, a network of cities all over Germany had agreed to build airship sheds from which the passenger line could operate.

There were many problems, at first, since reliable weather forecasts were not available. In the summer of 1911, during good weather, the German Airship Transport Company's LZ 10 made almost 100 flights without one serious problem. The LZ 10's passenger gondola resembled a first-class railroad car, complete with the day's finest passenger comforts.

While traveling aboard blimps in fine style became popular, the rigid design pioneered by von Zeppelin made it possible to construct huge airships. The biggest ever created was the Hindenburg, at 804 feet long and 135 feet in diameter. This craft could lift a total weight of about 235 tons and carried 50 passengers and a crew of 60, along with baggage, mail cargo, and a heavy load of fuel. The Hindenburg was much larger than a Boeing 747 and almost as large as the Titanic! None of today's blimps are nearly as big.

On two decks of the gondola the passengers lived in the style and comfort of the day's most lavish hotels. Eventually, the Hindenburg made routine crossings of the Atlantic in about 61 hours, cruising at 650 feet at about 80 miles per hour. While the promise of safe passenger airship travel seemed to have arrived, the Hindenberg, like many blimps before, fell victim to disaster. On May 6, 1937, at Lakehurst Naval Air Station, New Jersey, the Hindenburg was destroyed by fire in an attempt to land. Thirty-five of the 97 people on board were killed and the history of blimp passenger transport was forever changed.

By World War II, nonrigid, helium-filled balloons were being used for patrolling, hunting submarines, and escorting convoys (groups of ships). They were still huge targets, but almost none were shot down. After the war, the increasing use of helicopters and the great expense of building and maintaining blimps eventually halted their use.

While the history of blimps is one of great change, great success, and great disasters, today's modern blimps have the reliability and services that would make early blimp designers like Count von Zeppelin proud. Tiny one- and two-person hot-air blimps are used primarily for aerial photography. Larger nine- and ten-person vessels carry passengers for sight-seeing, or as TV camera platforms during news and sporting events, or as flying billboards for advertisements.

General Aircraft

Currently, American aviation can be classified into three areas: *military aviation*, commercial airline (including air mail and cargo service), and *general aviation*. Although helicopters and gliders fall into the category of general aviation, the vast majority of aircraft in this category are airplanes. These planes are generally smaller than those used by commercial airline companies and can use the shorter runways of private airports, open fields, deserted roads, or lakes for landing. Since these smaller aircraft can come and go when they need to and can land almost anywhere, they are used in business and commercial activities as well as for instruction and pleasure. Since World War I about 80% of all aircraft in the United States are used for general aviation purposes.

During the 1920s much of the American public was introduced to flying by watching the "flying gypsies," or "*barnstormers*." Who were they? In 1919 hundreds of military service pilots were released from duty after World War I; at the same time hundreds of airplanes made for the war were released for sale. One in particular, the Curtis JN-4 and JN-4D, or "*Jenny*" as it was affectionately called, cost the government $5000 to make, but was sold for only a few hundred dollars. The low price and availability made it a great buy for ex-military pilots. The Jenny was not the only barnstorming airplane, but was so popular that it became the primary trademark of the "flying gypsies." The Jenny, with two cockpits and two wings, had a 90HP engine with a cruising speed of 60 MPH. These ex-military airmen traveled across the United States and gave thousands of people their first ride in an airplane, for a small fee. This captured the interest of Americans and ensured the future of general aviation.

By the mid-1920s, though many accidents and deaths caused people to be fearful or nervous about flying, general aviation continued to grow. Many barnstormers went on to establish "fixed base" operations where services such as protective hangars, repair shops, and maintained runways would encourage the continued growth of general aviation.

The need for aircraft services grew quickly due to hundreds of young, inventive aviator entrepreneurs. There were few regulations or restrictions, so many new things were tried. Many valuable fee-based services were provided, such as surveying, photography, emergency services, scenic tours, and transporting sportsmen to remote regions for hunting.

One individual, Major Jack Savage, introduced himself to New York City by writing "Hello U.S.A." in chemical smoke in the sky with his airplane. (This is called skywriting.) An advertising executive spotted his writing in the sky and immediately signed the major to a $1000-a-day contract to do skywriting, advertising the cigarette company. Other uses for the airplane soon followed. Politicians, looking for votes, flew from city to city. Reporters and photographers followed close behind to report the events, or to cover other events, such as natural disasters. During the prohibition era, when it was illegal to sell alcohol, law enforcement officials used airplanes to look for rum-runners, who in turn used aircraft to avoid capture.

FUN FACTS

✔ Vampire bats live in Mexico and Central and South America. They do not feed on human blood, but do feed on the blood of sleeping cattle or livestock.

All through the 1920s and 1930s business or commercial aviation continued to expand as the speed and flexibility of flying improved. Many businesses, such as breweries, supply firms, petroleum corporations, and mining companies saw the advantage of flight and dozens owned their own airplanes.

Additionally, the agricultural community discovered that a pilot with a plane equipped for aerial dusting could cover 500 acres per hour—a task that would normally take days and an entire crew! The pilot could seed a flooded rice field or eradicate the boll weevil from a cotton field with a powdered insecticide, all for a fraction of the usual cost and time expenditure. A similar application in locating and fighting forest fires soon followed. "Smoke jumpers" were flown to a fire and dropped by parachute or landed in a field near remote fires to quell the blazes.

Later, aerial photography and surveying were used to map cities, for tax purposes and for other large projects. In Alaska, supported by several organizations including the Bureau of Fisheries, the Division of Roads, and the Department of Agriculture, airplane surveyors mapped 23,000 square miles of territory, much never seen by humans before! Later, the oil industry would also benefit by surveying routes for laying pipelines while the helicopter could be used to lay the pipes themselves. Again, the airplane could be used to monitor the line, once it was laid, saving huge amounts of time and energy.

As was mentioned, many areas of flying were developed following World War I and are still used today. There is risk in flying, so the *Federal Aviation Administration (FAA)* now regulates aviation practices much more closely than it did during the 1920s and 1930s. Other agencies and groups, such as the *National Transportation and Safety Board (NTSB)* and the Bureau of Aviation Safety, help monitor and regulate aviation safety.

To this day new uses for general aircraft are still being discovered. An executive flies to a meeting in New York on Monday and then to another meeting in a remote town in Alaska on Tuesday. Recently, on Mt. Everest, a helicopter pilot saved lives at an elevation never attempted before. In Wyoming a rancher located 11 stray cattle from his private airplane, and radioed his ranch hands to go get them. The same rancher dropped alfalfa bales to his cattle in a high pasture where the snow was too deep to bring them back. Off the coast of California an aerial spotter found a school of salmon and reported their location to a commercial fisherman nearby.

With a little imagination, you too can sit down and list ten, twenty, or thirty different uses of general aircraft.

Commercial Aircraft

Commercial aircraft can be defined as privately owned airplanes that offer a scheduled service to passengers and shippers of cargo. Most *commercial airplanes* are larger than general aircraft and are specially designed to carry passengers and/or cargo from one location to another on a regular schedule. Almost everyone in the world today has either seen or used the services of commercial airplanes. The public uses these airplanes to travel swiftly for a variety of purposes, ranging from business to vacation. Businesses also use commercial airplanes to ship their products around the world. There are thousands of airports throughout the world and tens of thousands of commercial airplanes in service. In fact, the commercial airline industry has grown from a few planes to a multibillion dollar industry in less than 90 years.

Commercial aviation dates back to 1910 and has evolved over the years from early primitive machines to that of today's modern supersonic transport planes. On June 22, 1910, the first regular passenger-carrying airship service began. On this day the firm of Delag operated an inter-urban, or city to city, service in Germany. In 1914 the St. Petersburg-Tampa, Florida, Airboat Line operated in the United States. In Russia the Il'ya Muromets flew from St. Petersburg, Russia, to Kiev and back to demonstrate the efficiency of a multi-engined transport airplane. Passenger carrying soon became an everyday event; night flying, seaplane flying, shipboard take-off and landings, long distance flying, airmail, parachuting and the formation of national air forces all began between 1910-1914. The ability of airplanes to carry cargo was the main driving force in the development of commercial airplanes at this time.

FUN FACTS

✔ There were six flights in Project Mercury, the series of flights that paved the way to the first American lunar landing. The names of the spacecraft were: Freedom 7, Liberty Bell 7, Friendship 7, Aurora 7, Sigma 7, and Faith 7. The "7" referred to the fact that there were 7 astronauts selected for Project Mercury.

By 1918 the United States Post Office had established an airmail service between New York and Washington. By 1920 this same service extended from New York to California! At first, the carriage of mail was the driving force of early commercial air transport. But the area of passenger travel soon supplied most of the progress and development of commercial aviation.

As commercial aviation developed, companies offered better, safer service at a lower cost. Flying had to be easy, safe, and comfortable for passengers. On passenger airplanes flight attendants serve meals, drinks, and tended to the requests of passengers. Passenger airplanes have lavatories, kitchens, music, in-flight movies, and recently, public telephones. Millions of people today depend on planes for quick, easy transportation. Businesses expect swift airmail service and safe, quick, reliable transport of merchandise every day. During the 1930s engineers made major improvements in commercial aviation. They made planes which were bigger, and could fly faster, further and higher; and could carry heavier loads than ever before. As planes flew higher, pressurized cabins were designed to make breathing at 35,000 feet as easy as at 6000 feet. Other improvements were controllable-pitch propellers, greatly improved onboard radio equipment, automatic pilots, and more accurate navigation. Airspeeds and seating capacity increased during the 1930s.

During the 1940s, jet engines were developed and improved. The world's first large commercial jet airliner, the de Havilland Comet, was built and flown in 1952. The de Havilland Comet flew nearly 500 MPH with little vibration or noise. But disaster struck when two exploded in flight. This caused stronger bodies for airliners to be developed. Flying times between London and Tokyo, using jet transportation, dropped from 85 hours with propeller-driven airplanes to 36 hours. Another development was the turboprop engines. Used by many small airlines, these engines are ideal for short and medium distances and are quieter and cheaper to build and run. Small jet aircraft can fly high, fast, and smooth, but are expensive to operate. Still, many clients are willing to pay the price.

While many engineering improvements were made, some things stayed the same. The main body of the plane, or the fuselage, is the familiar tube shape and contains the lavatories, galley, cargo bay, seating for passengers and crew, and the controls. Seating is usually first class up front with the more tightly packed "economy class" behind. Carry-on luggage is usually stored over the seats and larger items that are checked in are stored below in the "hold." The pilot and other crew sit on the flight deck at the front of the plane. The wings are located near the middle of the fuselage and are angled backward. Each wing supports one or two engines. Other features of the plane are a passenger door, cargo door, nose wheel, and landing gear and hydraulic system, which operates flying control surfaces, cargo doors, landing gear, and brakes. Additionally there are usually backup hydraulic systems in case of failure.

FUN FACTS

✔ Bats are very clean animals who groom their wings and teeth regularly.

Safety is a top priority. There is little room for error when an airplane is flying hundreds of people through the sky at over 500 miles per hour.

How fast will commercial flights travel? Planes that travel faster than the speed of sound are called "supersonic." The Soviet Union built the first supersonic cargo transport, but in 1976 Britain built the Concorde. The Concorde could travel 1450 miles per hour. It crossed the Atlantic in just under 3 hours! A 3480 mile flight! Although the Concorde was fast, it was also expensive to operate and lost a large amount of money in its first 5 years of service. New commercial airlines of today focus on fuel economy, quietness, and automation instead of speed. Greater safety, increased reliability, less noise and pollution, better passenger comfort, more navigational aids, and less room for pilot error are all guidelines for the commercial airplanes of tomorrow. There are about 200 major airlines worldwide. They carry more than 800 million passengers every year. To get an idea of the volume of traffic this represents, think about the Chicago O'Hare International Airport. This one airport has over half a million take-offs and landings every year. This represents an average of more than one take-off or landing every minute, 24 hours a day! Look how far commercial airlines have come since the early days of Orville and Wilbur Wright. There is little doubt that commercial aviation is here to stay.

FUN FACTS

✔ Apollo 12 was struck by lightning twice during its launch.

Military Aircraft

By 1908, Orville and Wilbur Wright demonstrated their "flying machine" to the United States Army. Around this same time military leaders in Italy, England, Germany, and France were also considering aviation for military purposes. Eventually, Italy became the first nation to take the airplane to war.

In 1910 the Italian Army purchased a few aircraft as an experiment. They used these on October 23, 1911, to fly over their enemy's army to see what they were doing. A few days later an Italian pilot dropped four hand grenades on Turkish troops. This was the first time that "bombs" had been dropped from an airplane on an enemy. Later another Italian soldier went up in an airplane and took the first pictures of an enemy army. Finally, Turkish troops shot down an Italian plane with rifle fire. Air warfare had now come full circle.

During the beginning of World War I, the airplanes were not all that sturdy. In the first months of war, Germany lost about 100 planes, mostly due to malfunctions and simple accidents.

These early airplanes had average speeds of about 60 miles per hour, flew at altitudes ranging from 3300 to 12,000 feet, and could stay in the air from 2 to 4 hours. Planes were used to photograph enemy positions, bomb the enemy, and sometimes to shoot at other planes in the air. Their design improved quickly because of the war.

After World War I several countries wanted to improve their air forces for the future. The creation of the aircraft carrier allowed military aircraft to be brought across the sea. Another innovation was the development of the long-range bomber, the Martin B-10. With twin engines and retractable gear the all-metal B-10 could fly up to 28,000 feet and hit speeds of over 200 miles per hour.

Through the 1930s, military air services began to develop modern planes with increased aerodynamic construction, retractable landing gear, heavier fire power, faster speeds, and better maneuverability. New engines and better radio contact also contributed to this progress.

By 1939, when the Second World War was beginning in Europe, the United States realized it was lagging behind other nations in its military air force. The United States only had 26,000 airmen and 1900 aircraft compared to Germany's half-million airmen and 4100 aircraft. In addition, the U.S. aircraft were inferior to German and English designs, with the possible exception of the B-17 Bomber.

With the encouragement of President Roosevelt, and millions of dollars from Congress, the United States soon made a firm commitment to improve American air power.

At the end of World War II, aircraft designers agreed that the future of aircraft was in jets, not piston engines. By 1951 aircraft design teams created the first jet fighter to exceed the speed of sound in level flight. By 1953 "Kelly" Johnson had outlined the Lockheed 83, an aircraft with a new J79 engine able to reach Mach 2 (twice the speed of sound).The year 1954 saw the XF-103 fighter fly at Mach 3.7, or 2447 miles per hour. The Chance Vought F-8 Crusader was the first carrier plane to fly faster than 1000 miles per hour. It also became the first plane to fly across the United States from the Atlantic to the Pacific Ocean at supersonic speed.

Above, the SR-71 "Blackbird." Below, the B-58 "Hustler."

In the 1960s the McDonnell F-4 Phantom was an even more advanced fighter. The Phantom claimed over one dozen world records for speed and rate of climb. The Convair B-58 Hustler became the world's first supersonic bomber, blazing over targets at Mach 2. The Boeing B-52 Stratofortress was an eight-engine bomber with a 6000 mile range that could be easily doubled with air-to-air refueling.

Surprisingly, in the first part of the Vietnam war the American forces used older propeller-driven airplanes from WWII and the Korean War. These were slower than jet aircraft but seemed to be less vulnerable (able to be hit) to ground fire. Helicopters became a powerful military vehicle during the Vietnam war. The helicopter could surprise the enemy by very quickly transporting infantry (ground soldiers) and artillery (big guns) to where the enemy was gathered. Helicopters could maintain remote outposts, provide rapid evacuation, withdraw troops, or bring wounded personnel to medical centers. Helicopters also carried weapons and evolved into "gunships."

Today, it takes several years for an airplane to be designed, tested, and manufactured. Sometimes the need for a particular plane will change or disappear. Also, the cost of making one airplane can be hundreds of millions of dollars. New designs and changes to existing aircraft will continue as long as there is a threat of war or military leaders feel national security requires it.

Experimental Aircraft

Ever since the Wright brothers first got off the ground, people have been trying to make bigger, better, and faster aircraft. To do this takes planning, money, building, and experimenting. Over the years this experimenting process has split into two divisions. The first category is centered around the *Experimental Aircraft Association (EAA)*. This is a group of flying enthusiasts whose main interest is designing and building their own flying machines. The second category is centered around professional research, mostly financed by the U.S. government and controlled by NASA (National Aeronautics and Space Association).

Each year the EAA sponsors an air show in Oshkosh, Wisconsin. This goes on for one week during the month of August. More than 500,000 people attend from around the world. Those days are spent browsing through the rows of airplanes on display around the grassy fields. Fellow builders and pilots exchange ideas and tips. This is called a "fly market" where all kinds of aviation-related memorabilia may be purchased. There are also exhibit halls where home-building suppliers sell everything from landing gear legs to upholstery and plans.

FUN FACTS

✔ There are more than 800,000 species of insects and still hundreds more are discovered every year.

The fun at Oshkosh wouldn't be complete without an airshow. Every afternoon some of the best-known pilots in the business put their aircraft through dazzling routines. There are pyrotechnic (fireworks) displays, mass fly-pasts, aerobatic routines, and various stunts that change from year to year. At this time of year the Oshkosh airport is the busiest in the world. The Oshkosh air show is a tribute to the love of flying by the thousands of EAA members.

Most of the aircraft built at home are built by one or two people over a long period of time for fun and recreation. The aircraft used by the military and commercial airlines must be built more quickly and pass much higher standards of flight and endurance. These are called "research" aircraft. Research airplanes are built to explore new areas in the science of flight or to learn how to design airplanes that will fly faster. Some are designed for learning how to develop airplanes that can take off from a space as small as a parking lot instead of a long runway.

Today, research aircraft are designed with the help of computers. The use of computers allows engineers to find out how a new or modified airplane will fly even before it is built. Once a good design is developed, a large-scale model of the real airplane may be built. After many tests the plane itself is built.

Flying a research plane is not easy or safe. Only the best, most highly trained pilots are candidates for the job. Years of hard work and millions of dollars are at stake. The test pilot must be able to feel every movement of the plane and sense potential problems immediately. If the first flight goes as planned, it will involve a simple take-off, a gradual climb, some easy maneuvers, and a modest landing. After a few such flights and careful checks by mechanics and engineers, the plane will be flown at its full performance levels.

Past research has centered around high-speed airplanes. The "sound barrier," 750 MPH at sea level and 650 MPH at high altitude, is what forced designers and engineers to build pure research airplanes. On October 14, 1947, Army Air Force Captain Charles E. (Chuck) Yeager flew the Bell XS-1 (later called the X-1) at 700 MPH, becoming the first person to fly faster than the speed of sound (Mach 1). Six years later, on November 20, 1953, test pilot Scott Crossfield flew an airplane at Mach 2 (1291 MPH).

Another area of research aircraft is that of the V/STOL (Vertical/Short Take Off and Landing) plane. This plane eliminates the need for long runways. It works both like an airplane and a helicopter. V/STOLS may be powered by propellers or jet engines. Such machines can take off straight up in the air or after only a very short stroll down a runway. They are very useful for supporting ground troops in battle.

When discussing research of airplanes, one must mention the NASA Dryden Flight Research Facility. Located on the western edge of the Mojave desert, it is the site of high-performance aeronautical flight research. This place has a 500-mile high-speed flight corridor and almost ideal weather. The Dryden Research

Center has become a huge success in pioneering aeronautical research.

The Dryden Research Center is now more than 50 years old and has been involved in the development and testing of many advanced aircraft, much of it leading to the development of the U.S. Space Shuttle program. Dryden is used as one of the landing areas of the space shuttle. After landing, the shuttles are serviced and carried back to Kennedy Space Center in Florida, piggyback atop the NASA 747 Shuttle Carrier Aircraft.

NASA's experimental vector thrust vehicle.

How was the space shuttle developed? Much of it came from the "X-plane projects." The *X-planes* began with the idea of designing an aircraft that could fly faster than the speed of sound. When this was accomplished, other projects began. X-1A, 1B, and 1D planes were made to fly higher than 90,000 feet and faster than Mach 2. The X-1E was created with thin wings and a more efficient engine turbo pump. The X-3 was designed for high-speed flight and control research and fitted with advanced aircraft tire technology. The X-5 was built to research variable-sweep wings while the X-9 carried and tested air-to-ground nuclear missiles (unarmed). Later X planes explored such areas as jet-powered vertical take-offs and landings.

FUN FACTS

✔ Insects have been flying for 250 million years!

The most successful of the X-planes, however, may be the X-15. First flown on September 17, 1959, the X-15 explored high-speed, high-altitude manned flight. The X-15 proved that manned flight near the Mach 5+ speed at altitudes over 250,000 feet was possible. Later, the X-15 would set an altitude record for aircraft at 317,750 feet and reach a top speed of Mach 6.7 (4520 MPH). The information gathered from the X-15 flights helped the U.S. space effort. The Mercury, Gemini, and Apollo spacecraft all used various X-15 technologies. The X-15 showed that going into space and returning to a horizontal landing on earth was possible and contributed to the design of the space shuttle.

Today, the engineers at Dryden are still designing and testing new technologies and new aircraft. For example: with the F-16XL engineers are testing new ways to make air flow more smoothly over an airplane so that fuel is more efficiently used. Additionally they are creating reusable launch vehicles designed to reduce space travel costs and are designing environmental research aircraft that are operated by remote control to gather information about our atmosphere.

With each of these projects, many new and difficult problems arise, which is to be expected in the field of experimental aircraft. For most modern aircraft, computer software is a necessity and in this field it has made more aircraft design and flight simulation possible.

In August 1996, NASA and the U.S. Air Force introduced a jet-powered aircraft equipped with state-of-the-art flight control technologies that showed a computerized flight control system that "learns" as it flies. These new systems are called "*neural networks.*" Neural networks are computer systems that actually learn by doing. The aircraft control system learns by mimicking the pilot. If all goes as planned, the program could eventually find its way into commercial, general, and military aircraft.

The field of aviation changes and improves through the efforts of amateur home-builders or by the work of the professional engineers working with research aircraft.

Spacecraft

Spacecraft include the rockets, *satellites*, unmanned and manned vehicles and structures that travel above the earth's atmosphere. Think about the spacecraft that you know about, like the space shuttle or a weather satellite. Unlike airplanes, most spacecraft have missions that are much longer in length. Satellites are meant to stay in orbit for years! The shuttle astronauts stay in space for about a week. Astronauts that have missions on a space station typically stay there for a few months. Can you imagine being on an airplane for a few months? Their design and function are completely different.

Unmanned vehicles such as small probes and satellites are used for exploration or communications. They carry instruments to conduct studies and report results back to earth. They circle around the earth and travel to other planets.

An unmanned satellite.

Satellites are used in weather detection. They are estimated to have saved many lives and billions of dollars due to the weather information they provide. They have also been used to detect oil slicks, diseases (Lyme disease), assist real estate development, study crop health, and update aerial maps.

Manned vehicles include the space shuttle. There are also space structures like the space stations.

The early rockets which carried fireworks were "solid propellent" rockets. These rockets used powder for fuel. Scientists realized that these rockets were not powerful enough to lift anything into space. The scientists could not control the fuel consumption or navigation. They knew that these types of rockets might not be very safe for human travel.

Liquid chemical fuels and gases like oxygen were being developed. Unlike propulsion systems for air-breathing engines, rockets needed to carry all of their fuel with them. On earth, oxygen is the oxidizer for most engines. In space you have to bring the oxidizer with you! Engineers could control the amount of fuel released with liquid fuels.

There were many other challenges. The materials the rocket engine and fuel containers were made out of had to be able to withstand heat, high pressure, and very cold conditions.

Professor Robert Goddard was the first person to launch successfully a liquid propellent rocket, in 1926. After World War II, a group of German scientists that had worked on the V-2 missile came to the United States. They worked with the U.S. government and developed multistage rockets. One rocket would be mounted on top of another to gain more altitude and speed.

The rockets became larger and larger, but what would they carry into space? What would be the first thing you would send into space?

The first objects sent into space were unmanned vehicles. This made a great deal of sense and is still a practice used in the space program today. First, information is gathered with satellites and instruments. The information collected is analyzed and used to develop safe methods and equipment that are later used to design spacecraft for manned missions.

Rockets are meant to get vehicles into space. Once that is done, the rocket has served its purpose. Satellites and other vehicles are meant to remain in space. Sometimes they are meant to stay there forever like satellites, probes, and space stations. Other vehicles like the space shuttle are "reusable" vehicles. They are meant to fly into space, return home safely, and then go into space again on another mission.

The space shuttle in the United States has been used to carry astronauts and scientists into space to conduct many experiments, particularly in little gravity, or "microgravity." Medical experiments are conducted to study the effects of space travel on living beings. How long can humans stay in space? Will there be any long-term effects that can harm people once they return to earth? Shuttle astronauts also launch and repair satellites!

Space shuttle missions last about one week. So the space shuttle has a cockpit like an airplane, living quarters for the astronauts, and an area to conduct science experiments.

Yet, even a week may not be long enough to study how well humans can adjust to space flight. A manned mission to Mars will take 3 years. Can humans survive that? Once in space the body adjusts to low gravity conditions. The fluids in your body actually redistribute themselves. Your waist, face, and hands change size! On earth, your body gets a lot of exercise just from walking every day. In space you float, you don't use your leg muscles very much. The muscles become weak. Astronauts have special machines to help them exercise in space. But what will happen after 3 years in space?

To study these long-term effects on people, astronauts need to stay in space a longer time. Space stations, which are about the size of a small house, provide the kind of environment where astronauts can live for months at a time.

On both the space shuttle and in the space stations there is no "ceiling." All walls can be used. Everything floats in space. Everything must be secured in a safe place or else it can damage something or hurt someone. The astronauts do not lay down in beds. They sleep in sleeping bags and attach themselves to the walls so that they do not float into something.

Although there have been many types of airplanes, there have only been a few types of spacecraft so far. There is no telling what the future will hold. How would you design a spacecraft? What would its mission be? Where would it go? What kind of propulsion system could you use? What kind of materials will be used? Do you have a future in space?

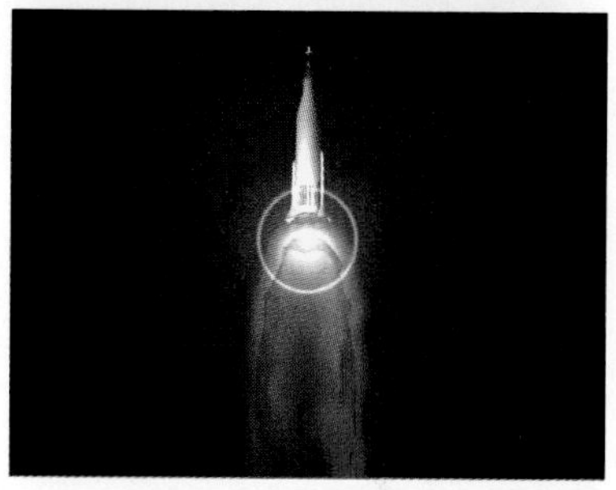

The space shuttle is transported "piggyback" on top of a Boeing 747.

Kite Flying

60–90 minutes

MATERIALS

- 4 wooden skewers or 4 straight drinking straws
- tissue paper
- 1 sheet colored construction paper, poster size
- 1 yard of light-weight cloth like rip-stop nylon
- ball of string or ribbon
- glue
- safety scissors
- stapler
- balsa wood (found at most craft or hobby shops)
- tagboard or poster board
- clay for weight
- Styrofoam paper plates
- paper clips
- rubber band launcher made from pencil and heavy rubber band

STEPS TO FOLLOW:

1 **How do you construct a kite? Decide on a shape or form by drawing a few different designs. Feel free to check out books on kites from your library for this purpose. Kites come in various shapes and forms, but the basic forms are: flat or *bowed*, box or cellular, and *semirigid* or *nonrigid*.**

2 **Design the sticks and frames for the kite, cutting them to the appropriate length. The frame should be strong but light weight.**

3 **Choose a strong but light cover material.**

4 **Choose how you will stabilize your kite. Will you attach a tail or a wind cup which catches the air and acts as a stabilizing anchor? You can make a tail out of paper, ribbon, or material. A wind cup can be fashioned from the same material as the rest of the kite.**

5 **Will you *vent* your kite? To vent, create openings in the material of the kite using scissors. Venting allows some air to go through the material, adding stability to some kites.**

6 **When you get ready to launch your kite, make sure you are in an area that is open and free from trees, electrical and telephone lines, buildings and automobile traffic. Stand with your back to the wind. Hold the kite with one hand and the reel of string with the other. Let the wind lift the kite and as it does, feed out the line to the height you wish. Walk in the direction of the wind as you feed out the line. Make adjustments in control surfaces to demonstrate how it behaves differently.**

SCIENCE EXPLANATION:

For a kite to fly, the air lift potential must be greater than the weight of the kite. Also, knowing the strength of the wind and wind direction are useful in developing a knowledge of the basic moves and tricks in kite flying.

The tail of a kite adds to its stability and balance. It also increases drag, and for some kites will limit the maximum altitude that can be reached. In designing kites, the pros and cons to each element of design must be weighed. For example, one can eliminate the tail, but bow out the design for stability and thus achieve greater altitude.

Tissue Balloons

60 minutes

MATERIALS

- tissue paper
- glue
- safety scissors
- hair dryer

STEPS TO FOLLOW:

1 **Glue sheets of tissue together at the top edges to make approximately 2-foot lengths. You will need eight, 2-foot lengths. Stack together.**

2 **Trace a petal shape onto the top 2-foot length of tissue.**

3 **Do the same for each 2-foot length of tissue, until you have cut out eight petal shapes.**

4 **Glue the edges of all the petal shapes together to make a balloon shape. Use glue very sparingly.**

5 **Strengthen the balloon by gluing a collar of tissue around the opening and a circle of tissue to the top to reinforce the seams and keep air from escaping.**

6 **Inflate the balloon with a hair dryer. Observe. (The balloon will rise.)**

SCIENCE EXPLANATION:

Heat warms the air around the earth, causing changes in atmospheric conditions: temperature, density, and pressure. You will discover that warm air can make an object rise. As air is warmed, its molecules spread out. This makes the air lighter, and it rises. As the air in the tissue balloon is warmed, it expands and rises. The rising warm air fills the balloon and causes it to rise also. Try this experiment with the cold air setting on the hair dryer; you'll observe that the balloon does not stay in the air.

Parachutes

STEPS TO FOLLOW:

1 **Wrap and tie each bag handle securely to the arms or other part of the small toy. Start making the knot in the bag and slip the arm of the action figure or other part of the toy into the knot before tightening it.**

2 **Grab the bottom of the bag and squeeze all the air out. Wrap the bag around your hand until it forms a small bundle. Slip your hand out from the bundle.**

3 **Outdoors, throw (underhand-style) the whole bundle straight up as high as you can. Your parachute should float down.**

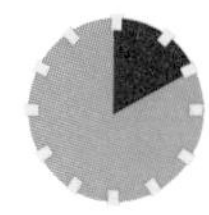

10 minutes

MATERIALS

- plastic grocery bag (with handles)
- small toy action figure or other small toy (less than 6 inches) or plastic film canisters partially filled with sand

SCIENCE EXPLANATION:

Air forced the parachute to fill. It opened the parachute. Air resistance or drag holds a parachute open and allows it to fall slowly. Air is trapped under the "dome," creating enough resistance to slow a parachute down.

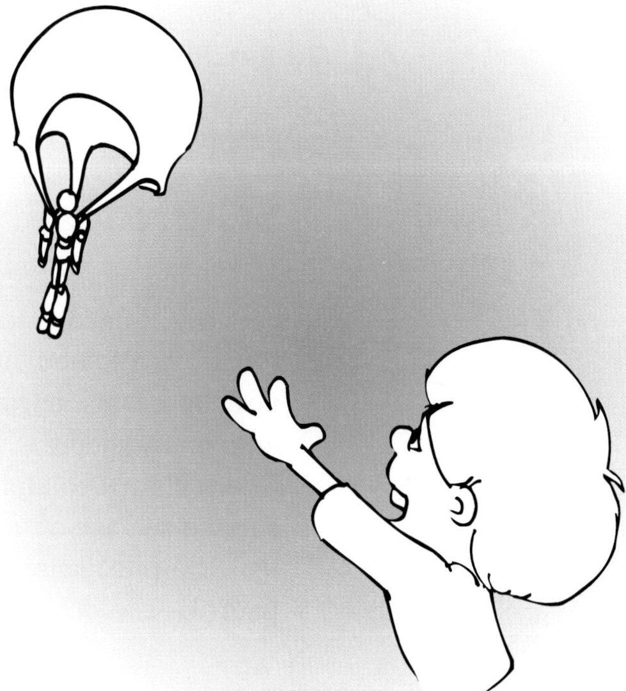

Balsa Wood Glider

2 hours

MATERIALS

- balsa wood (select sizes that are close to the shapes in the pattern included. Balsa wood can be found at most craft or hobby shops)
- heavy plastic gloves
- steel wool
- safety scissors
- heavy-duty sandpaper
- pencils and paper
- paint and paint brushes (optional)

STEPS TO FOLLOW:

1 **Photocopy the glider pattern at right, or look through other books on flight and copy the gliders in them.**

2 **Draw your design onto the balsa wood. Press down hard enough with the pencil so that you can easily see the outline of the glider on the wood.**

3 **Cut the glider out using scissors.**

4 **Put on the gloves. Using the steel wool and heavy-duty sandpaper, shape the glider rounding all the edges until they match the model pattern you have chosen. You'll need to be patient using the steel wool, but it does work on the balsa wood.**

5 **Once your glider is shaped, paint it and let it dry.**

6 **Go outside and fly your glider. Move the wings from side to side and see how it flies.**

SCIENCE EXPLANATION:

Gliding could certainly be considered a subdued version of aerobatics—a dance with the atmosphere. Most often towed into the sky by another plane (some now have small engines to relieve this necessity), pilots who enjoy gliding use thermals to lengthen their flights. Thermals are columns of hot air rising from the earth's surface and are often capped by clouds. Once in a thermal, the pilot spirals the plane until the thermal dissipates or the desired elevation is reached.

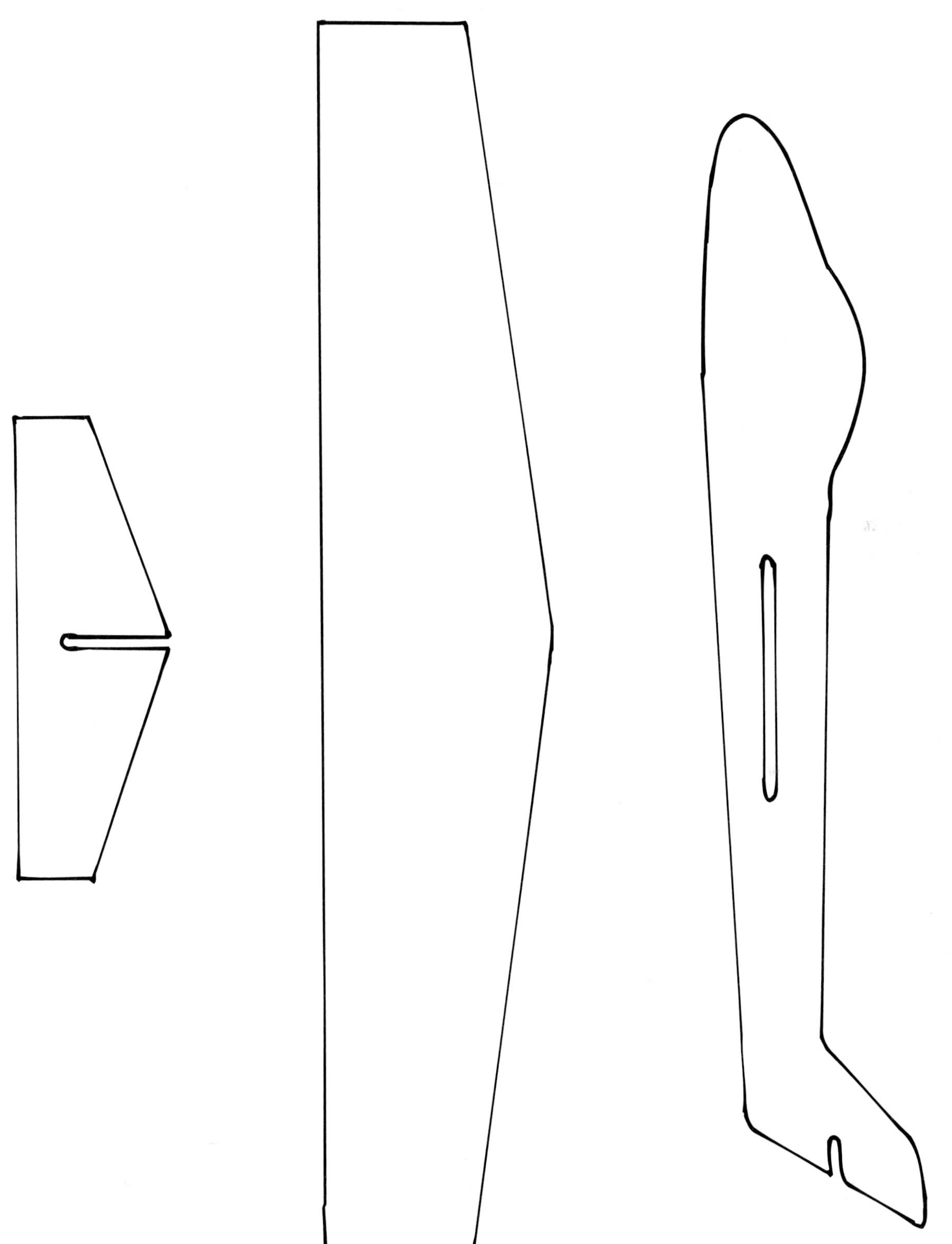

Edible Aircraft

30–60 minutes

MATERIALS

- long cookies
- wafer cookies
- crackers
- ice cream cone
- straight thick long pretzel sticks
- marshmallows
- toaster tarts
- straight thin pretzel sticks
- licorice sticks
- gum drops
- thick white cookie icing
- tooth picks (optional)

STEPS TO FOLLOW:

1 **Use the long cookies or toaster tarts to make the wings of your biplane or other airplane.**

2 **Use the thin pretzel sticks or licorice for the wires and spars of your airplane. (You may have to munch on the pretzel sticks or the licorice to make them all the same length!)**

3 **Hold them in place with the thick icing until dry.**

4 **Use crackers, cookie wafers, or biscuits for the rudder and elevator. Use the icing to connect them to the airplane with the licorice or pretzels.**

5 **Use gumdrops as the propeller hub and long pretzel sticks as the blades. Attach them with icing.**

6 **Use an ice cream cone for the nose of the Concorde. Use marshmallows or gumdrops for its tires.**

7 **Let the icing dry.**

SCIENCE EXPLANATION:

Building models teaches us about the shapes and function of the components of air and space vehicles. Can you imagine constructing a full-scale model?

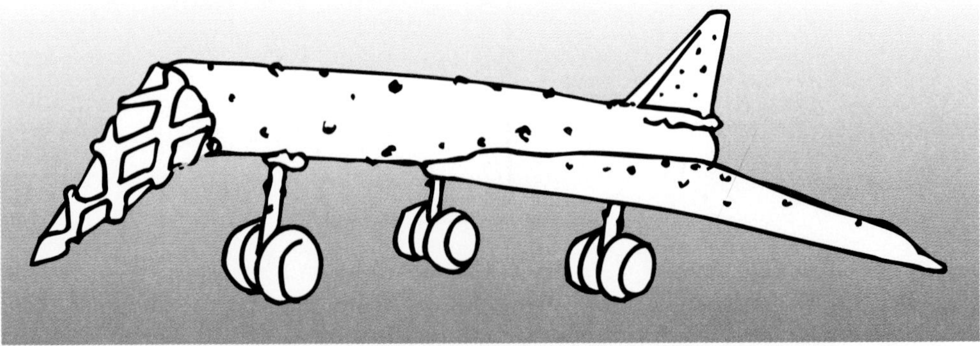

Feeling the Pressure

STEPS TO FOLLOW:

1 **Take the plastic cup and fill it halfway with water. Add a drinking straw.**

2 **Suck some water up into the straw and quickly cover the top of the straw with your finger so that water is trapped in the straw.**

3 **Lift the straw out of the plastic cup. What happens? (Nothing.) No air can get into the top to allow the water to come out.**

4 **Next, lift your finger off the straw. What happens now? Now the air can get into the top of the straw, and the water can flow out because of gravity.**

MATERIALS

- straws
- plastic cup
- water

SCIENCE EXPLANATION:

Since air has weight, it is held to the earth by the force of gravity, just as you are. Since gravity is strongest near the earth's surface, it holds most of the air, or atmosphere, close to the earth's surface. This pushing force of the air is called air pressure, and the closer to the earth you are, the greater the air pressure. You will explore air pressure using a drinking straw experiment and how gravity exerts its greatest strength near the earth's surface.

The higher you go in altitude, the less air pressure there is. When the astronauts are on the space shuttle there is no gravity, so they cannot suck water up a regular straw. Astronauts have special straws with clamps on them because there is little gravity to hold the water in the straw by air pressure.

In outer space, we become weightless. Astronauts experience different things because of this weightlessness—floating in air, being able to bounce along like a kangaroo when "walking," and needing special instruments to eat, "take showers," and go to the bathroom. That is why the straw in outer space is designed differently than the straw you will find in your own kitchen.

Nose and Wings of Aircraft

60 minutes

MATERIALS

- Box of junk including (but not limited to):
- clay
- straws
- safety scissors
- popsicle sticks
- paper clips
- index cards
- string
- empty thread spool
- Styrofoam trays
- toilet paper tubes
- plastic milk jug
- paper
- aluminum foil
- soft drink lid
- clear plastic tape
- rubber bands
- toothpicks
- glue
- balsa wood scraps
- vegetables – like potatoes, eggplant or zucchini, carrot
- paint

STEPS TO FOLLOW:

1 **Take pictures of airplanes and spacecraft from this book or others. Try to select pictures of vehicles that fall into each of these categories: general aviation, commercial aviation, military aircraft, experimental aircraft, and at least two space vehicles (like the space shuttle and the early spacecraft of the 1960s).**

2 **Look through the man-made flyers chapter. Classify the noses and wings of the vehicles into the following categories:**

How fast do they fly?

How high do they go?

Are they reusable? (This will be an important consideration for spacecraft.)

3 **Model the noses and wings (if any) of the vehicles using the supplies at left. (Vegetables make fun fuselages).**

SCIENCE EXPLANATION:

A fighter jet and the supersonic commercial jet, the Concorde, have sharp noses and wings. They fly at the speed of sound—Mach 1. They look fast! They look streamlined and aerodynamic.

The space shuttle flies much faster. The Apollo capsule that went to the moon flew at Mach 36—thirty-six times the speed of sound. But they look very different. The shuttle has a blunt nose. The Apollo capsule doesn't have wings at all and has a very blunt body that faces the earth during re-entry. Why would such a fast vehicle look so different? The faster the vehicle travels, the more it must withstand the effects of air friction. That friction creates extremely high temperatures on the surface of the vehicle. It is so hot that if a spacecraft did have a sharp nose, it would burn off. That is one reason why hypersonic vehicles have blunt noses.

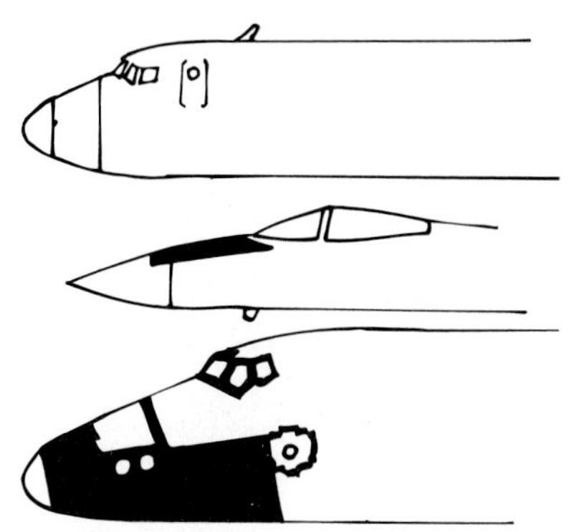

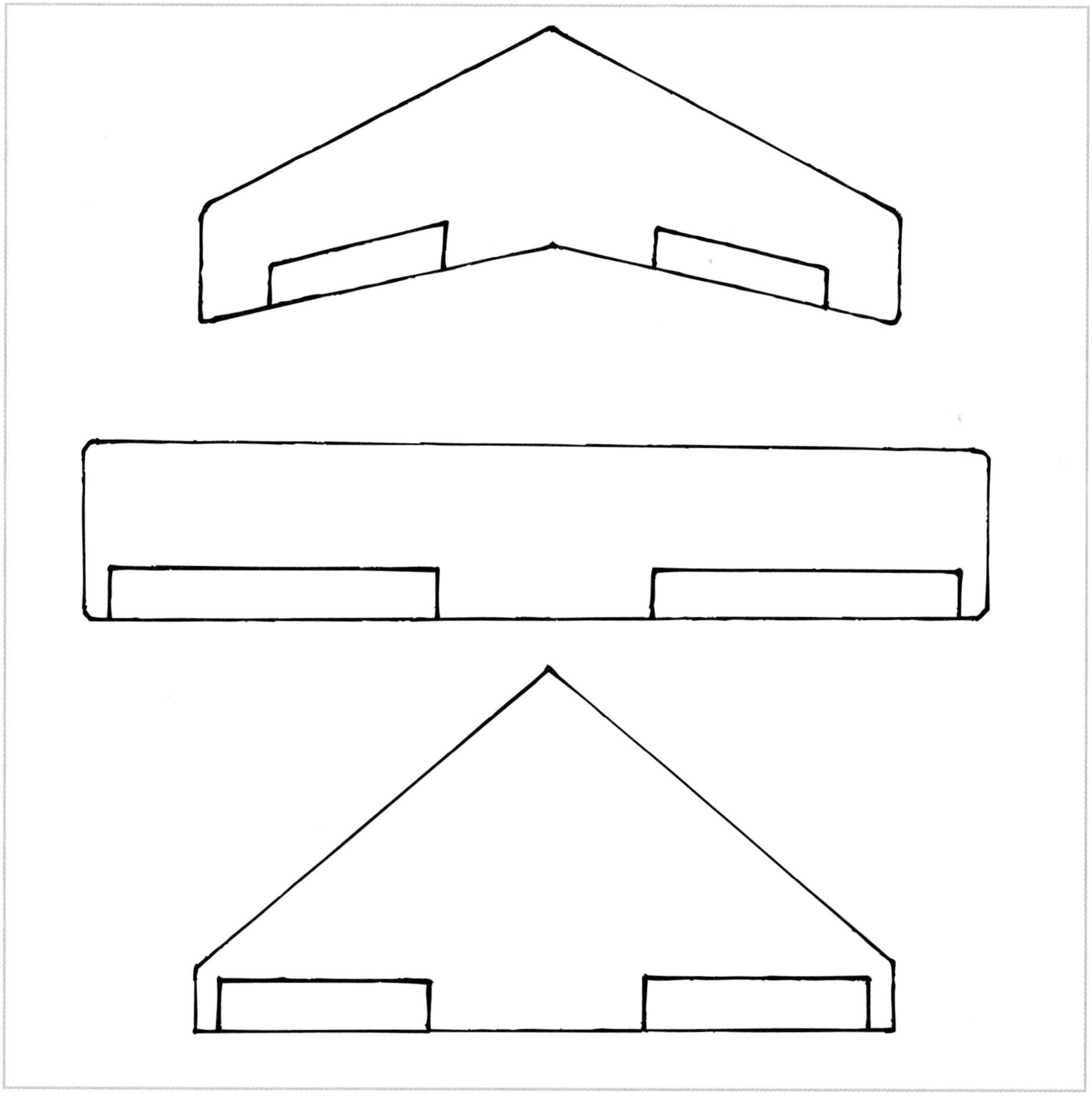

Remote Sensing

MATERIALS

- shoe box
- pencils or wooden skewers
- small solid objects that will fit in the bottom of the box

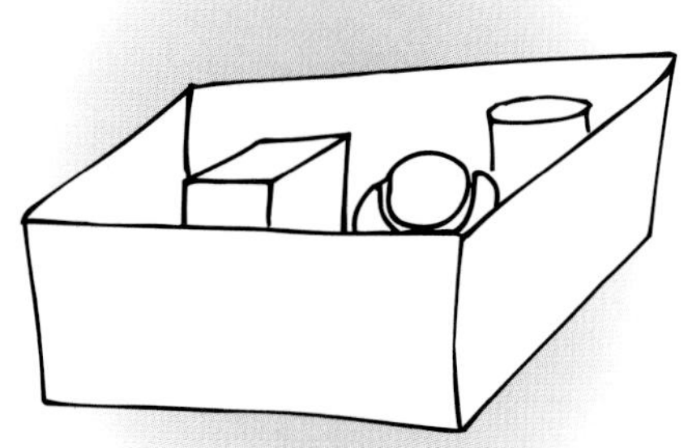

STEPS TO FOLLOW:

1 **Punch holes into the top of the shoe box with the pencils or wooden skewers, spacing them evenly. Keep the pencils or sticks at the same height.**

2 **Place small solid objects in the bottom of the box.**

3 **Place the top of the shoe box back on the box. Push the sticks gently into the box. Stop pushing when you touch an object in the box.**

SCIENCE EXPLANATION:

In this activity you will create an instrument that can help you determine the shapes of objects.

How do satellites map land or sea floors? One way is to send signals out that will tell them how far away an object is. The satellite can send a signal. Depending on how much time it takes for the signal to return, scientists can determine the distance to that object. By doing this over a wide area, they can determine the patterns of objects.

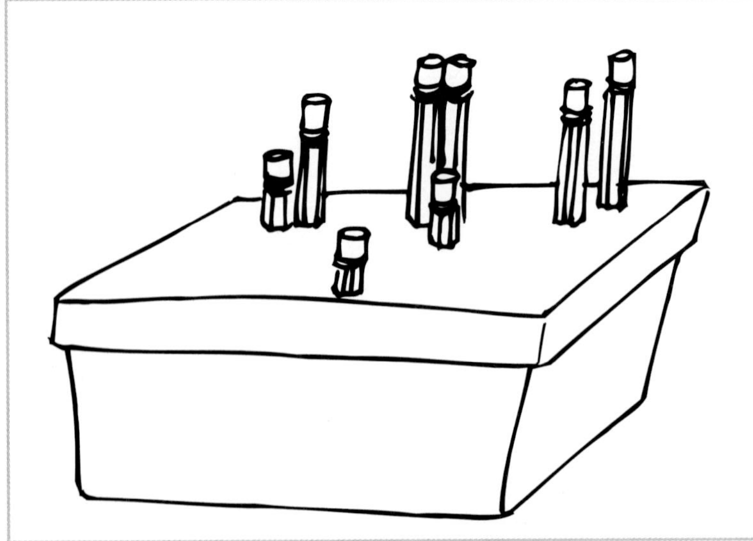

By pushing the pencils or sticks into the box, you obtained a "map" of the bottom of the box. The more pencils or sticks you used, the better the map you created. The pattern made by the top of the pencils or sticks resembles the "floor" of the box. Were you able to determine what shapes were at the bottom of the box?

The Space Station

STEPS TO FOLLOW:

1. **To construct the space station, look at the pictures in this activity. Study the different components of the space stations. You will build a model of a space station. You will need to consider that the space station needs power, docking facilities for visiting spacecraft, a system for communications, living quarters, and a science laboratory.**

2. **Using the materials listed to the right or others that you can think of or find around the house, construct a model of one of the space stations. Use your imagination.**

SCIENCE EXPLANATION:

The space stations have been more than a place to live and study the long-term effects of space on humans. They have also been a place to work and conduct scientific research.

When you build the space station model you'll realize that it's different than just building an air or space vehicle. It's much more. You will need to build a small community that can exist isolated from the rest of civilization.

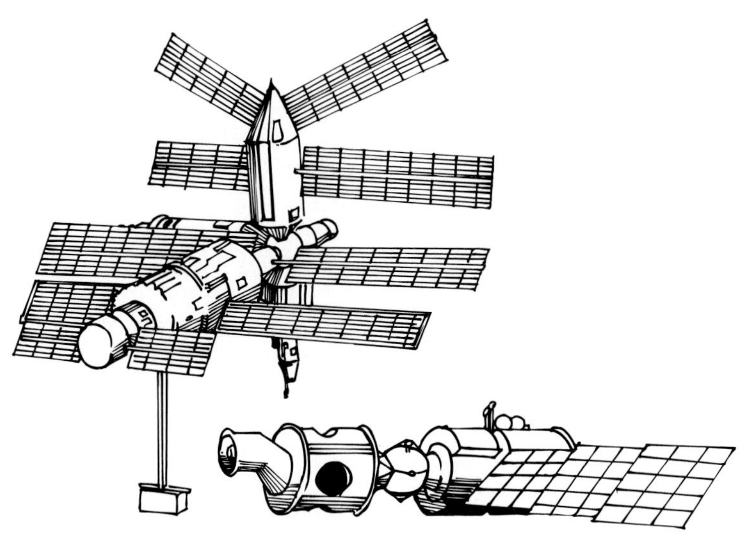

60 minutes

MATERIALS

- glue
- straight or bending drinking straws
- safety scissors
- plastic containers and tops that can be thrown away
- construction paper
- strawberry baskets
- egg carton
- aluminum foil
- velcro
- empty toiletpaper tubes
- shoe box
- cardboard
- cellophane tape
- clay
- action or small soldier figures
- pencils
- a roll of clear fishing line
- paper cups
- thread spool

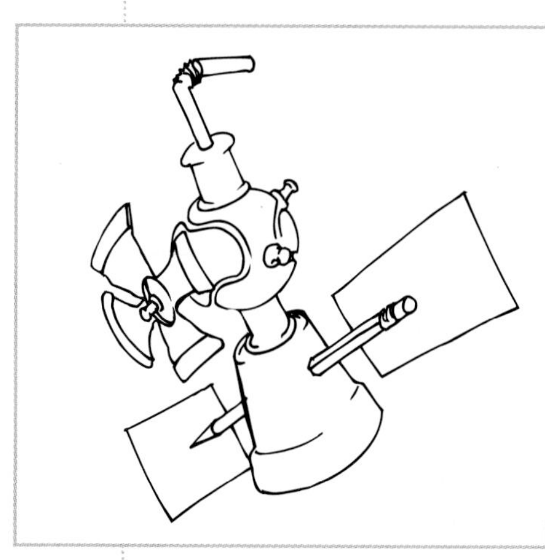

GLOSSARY

A

Acceleration: Rate of change in the velocity.

aerodynamicist: A person who studies aerodynamics.

aerodynamics: The study of the motions and forces of gases on an object.

aerodynes: Air vehicles which overcome the force of gravity through lift.

aeronautics: The science and technology of air flight.

aeronauts: The name given to the first balloonists.

aerospace: Relating to the region of the earth's atmosphere and outer space.

afterburner: A section of a propulsion system which provides additional thrust by burning fuel with the uncombined oxygen from the engine's exhaust.

ailerons: Located on the wings of an aircraft, ailerons help in banking or turning the aircraft.

airfoil: A cross-section of a wing.

alloy: A mixture of metals.

altitude: Elevation above the earth's sea level.

angle of attack: The angle the leading edge of an object is pitched or tilted.

area: The measure of the surface of an object.

astronautics: Science and technology of space flight.

astronauts: Literally means "star sailor"; the name given to Americans who travel into space; Soviet astronauts are called cosmonauts.

atmospheric pressure (air pressure): The force over a given area that the atmosphere or air creates.

attenuated: Slender and tapered.

axes: An imaginary line an object rotates about.

B

banking: Turning an aircraft.

barbs and barbules: Fine filaments projecting from the shaft of a feather.

barber chair: Nickname for the astronauts' adjustable seats in the early space.

barnstormers: Nickname for the military service pilots who continued to fly privately after World War I.

Bernoulli's Theorem: Aerodynamic law which states that an increase in velocity over a body is accompanied by a decrease in pressure and that a decrease in velocity is accompanied by an increase in pressure.

biplane: An airplane with two sets of wings. The 1903 Wright Flyer was a biplane.

bivalve: A shelled mollusk, like a scallop or clam.

boron: A soft, brown, nonmetallic element used in fabricating composites.

boundary layer: Layers of fluid that develop against a surface, each with less friction and a little faster velocity, until some distance away from the original surface the remaining layers of the fluid travel at the original velocity.

bowed: Curved or bent downward.

bridle: A harness attached to a kite used to guide and control it; it is secured at both ends of the kite and then a line is dropped down from its center point.

buoyancy: Principle discovered by Archimedes relating to the capacity an object has to float in a liquid or rise in a gas, like air.

C

cambered: Curved.

chiroptera: Animal order of bats; Greek for the word hand-wing.

center of gravity: Position where the resultant force of the earth's gravitational pull is concentrated.

combustor: The part of an engine which burns the fuel.

commercial airplane: Privately owned airplanes that offer a scheduled service to passengers and shippers of cargo.

composite materials: Materials made by bonding two or more materials together.

compressed: Pressed or squeezed together.

compression stress: An applied force that compresses.

compressor: The part of an engine which compresses gases.

Concorde: A commercial supersonic aircraft.

control: The ability to maneuver a vehicle; also is the science of flying and handling an aircraft.

cosmonauts: Literally means "cosmos sailor"; the name given to Soviets who travel into space.

D

deflection: Turn or bend.

deformable: Able to alter the shape.

density: Measure of mass (the amount of molecules) in a given object or volume.

dirigible: A motorized balloon, also known as a blimp. The motor allows the pilot to steer the vehicle and control the direction of the flight.

dorsoventrally compressed: Flattened top to bottom.

drag: Fluid resistance that slows the motion of an object.

duck pack: Cloth storage container for a parachute.

dynamic stability: The condition that an object does return to its original position after a motion is applied.

dynamically unstable: The condition that an object does not return to its original position after a motion is applied.

E

EAA: The Experimental Aircraft Association. A group of flying enthusiasts whose main interest is designing and building their own flying machines.

eddy: Current of air or water moving against the main flow in a circular direction.

elasticity: Ability of a material to deform.

elevator: The horizontal flaps on the tail assembly of an airplane; elevators cause the nose of the airplane to point up or down.

epoxy: An adhesive.

envelope: The skin of a blimp.

equilibrium position: The original position an object returns to after motion is applied.

F

FAA: The Federal Aviation Administration, which regulates aviation practices.

firewalls: Fireproof walls used to prevent the spread of fire.

flow separation: A condition where the air traveling over a surface no longer remains attached to that surface.

fluid: A liquid or a gas.

fluid dynamics: The study of the motion of a liquid or gas.

flying angle: The angle an object is flying relative to the wind.

force: Pushes or pulls on an object. Something that propels a body or changes its movement or direction.

form drag: Also called pressure drag. An aerodynamic force affected by the shape of the body. A smooth, streamlined shape will generate less form drag than a blunt or flat body.

friction: Resistance to motion, or the force between two objects that rub against one another.

friction drag: Also known as skin friction drag, the resistance to a fluid caused by surface roughness.

fuselage: Main body of an aircraft where the passengers and crew sit; the wings and tail of the aircraft are attached to the fuselage.

fusiform: Torpedo-shaped.

G

gas dynamics: Study of how high-speed gases change.

general aviation: Privately owned airplanes, helicopters, and gliders generally smaller than those used by commercial airline companies, and which can use the shorter runways of private airports, open fields, deserted roads, or lakes for landing.

glider: An engineless flying machine with fixed, non-flapping wings.

gondola: A box or cabin that is attached underneath the blimp.

gravity: The natural attraction that pulls objects back to the earth.

H

hydrodynamics: The study of how forces (pushes and pulls) affect liquids.

hydrofoil: Cross-section of a marine animals' flipper; also a winglike blade shape to lift the hull of the boat out of the water as the boat moves, thus reducing drag.

hydroplane: An aircraft with the ability to take-off and land on water.

hypersonics: The study of gas motion or flight over the speed of Mach 5.

I

I-beams: Structural supports that are shaped like the letter "I".

incompressible: Not able to make more compact by pressing together.

induced drag: Drag due to lift.

inlet: The opening of an engine which allows air to enter.

J

Jenny: The Curtis JN-4 and JN-4D airplane which was sold for a few hundred dollars after World War I.

jet propulsion (marine life): The ability to expel water and propel in the opposite direction.

K

keel: A rigid frame along the bottom of the blimp.

L

laminar boundary layer: A boundary layer which has smooth and orderly flow, without mixing.

lateral: Sideways.

laterally compressed: Flattened side to side.

length: The measure of how long an object is.

lift: One of the four aerodynamic forces that govern flight; it is the ability to rise in the air.

loading: Stress.

longitudinal: Over the length of the airplane.

M

Mach number: The ratio of the speed of an object to the speed of sound (Mach 2 is two times the speed of sound).

mammals: Warm-blooded animals that nurse their young.

maneuver: A movement or direction to change the flight path of an aircraft.

marine: Relating to the sea.

mass: A measure of how much of the substance is there—how many molecules and what type.

microgravity: Very low gravity.

military aviation: Aircraft used for military purposes, such as warfare, transportation, or surveillance.

monoplanes: Single-wing planes without struts and wires sticking out.

N

NACA: The National Advisory Committee on Aeronautics; government agency formed by President Woodrow Wilson to advance the United States progress in civil and military aviation.

nacelle: Outer covering of the engine.

NASA: The National Aeronautics and Space Administration. United States government agency which replaced NACA in 1958. NASA's mission is advance aeronautics and space exploration.

negative lift: Lift directed downward, as in a race car.

neural network: Computer systems that actually learn by doing. For example, an aircraft control system learns by mimicking the pilot.

Newton's Laws: Three laws of motion which state: 1) that a body will remain at rest until acted on by a force, 2) the definition of a force, 3) for every action there is an equal and opposite reaction.

non-deformable: Shape will not deform.

nonrigid: Flexible.

nozzle: The part of an engine which directs the exhaust.

NTSB: National Transportation and Safety Board; a government agency which helps monitor and regulate aviation safety.

O

orbital velocity: The speed needed to keep an object in orbit. The orbital velocity for the earth is 18,000 miles per hour.

outlet: The opening of an engine which allows gases to exit.

oxidizer: A chemical that mixes with fuel to create combustion.

P

payload: Equipment carried on a spacecraft or rocket.

pectoral fins: Fins located on the chest of a marine animal.

pitch: One of the three axes of motion for an aircraft; pitch moves the nose of the aircraft up or down.

power plant: Engine system.

pressure: Force over a specified area.

pressure drag:: Also known as form drag, the resistance to a fluid caused by the shape of an object.

propellant: Something, such as fuel, which propels or provides thrust.

propulsion: A method of movement; engines are a propulsion system.

pterosaurs: The first prehistoric animals to fly.

R

ram-jet: A type of engine with an inlet, a burner, and a nozzle meant for flight over the speed of sound.

GLOSSARY

reaction thrust principle: An application of Newton's Third Law; exhaust gases flow out the back of the engine, causing a reaction force on the airplane, pushing it forward.

roll: One of the three axes of motion for an aircraft; roll raises the wings of the aircraft up or down.

rudder: The vertical flap on the tail assembly, used to turn the airplane.

S

satellites: Unmanned vehicles used for space exploration or communications.

scramjet: Supersonic combustion ramjet.

semirigid: Partially flexible.

shear stress: A stress which occurs when layers of atoms try to slide across each other sideways.

shock wave: Cone-shaped area formed around the plane as it flies at supersonic speeds or faster. The pressure, density, temperature, and velocity of the air changes dramatically and immediately through a shock wave.

shrouds: Suspension lines on a parachute which connect the canopy to a ring on the harness.

six degrees of freedom of motion: The six directions an aircraft can move.

sonic boom: Loud explosive sound caused by an object breaking the sound barrier.

sound barrier: Mach 1; the sonic region.

spars: Structural member in a wing or a tail on an aircraft.

speed of sound: How fast sound waves travel; about 760 miles per hour (MPH) at sea level.

stability (for aircraft): The ability to resist change in direction and even restore itself to the original course.

stall: Advanced flow separation on a wing resulting in a loss of lift.

static stability: When you move an object and it returns to its original position.

stiffened shells: A curved object with varying shaped pieces of metal welded to the back side to strengthen it.

stiffened plates: A flat object with varying shaped pieces of metal welded to the back side to strengthen it.

streamlined: Designed to provide the least fluid resistance.

structures: The science which deals with how the plane is built and with what materials. Aircraft structural design is different from other structural fields, such as buildings or ships, because the plane must be both lightweight and strong, able to stay together even through gusts of wind or flying at very high speeds.

subsonic: Velocity less than the speed of sound; less than Mach 1.

supersonic: Velocity faster than the speed of sound; faster than Mach 1.

symmetric wings: Shaped such that the top and bottom surfaces are identical.

T

takeoff weight: The total weight of the plane, including the aircraft itself, plus the passengers, crew, baggage and freight, and the fuel at take-off.

temperature: A measure of how hot or cold something is.

thermals: Warm air currents which assist in gliding flight.

thrust: One of the four aerodynamic forces that govern flight; thrust is the power to move through the air.

time: A measure of how long it takes for something to happen.

trailing edge: Back edge of a wing.

transition region: The area where the orderly laminar layers start to mix together, but before they become turbulent.

transonic: Velocity between Mach 0.75 and Mach 1.20; vehicles flying at this speed will experience both subsonic and supersonic effects.

truss: A framework of beams or bars used to support a structure.

turbine: A machine that converts the kinetic energy of a moving fluid to mechanical power.

turbofan: An engine which is a compromise between the turboprop and the turbojet engines.

turbojet: The original jet engine composed of an inlet, a compressor, a combustor, a turbine, and a nozzle.

turboprop: A jet engine created to be more fuel efficient at lower speeds. This engine design produces two thrusts, one with the propeller and the other through exhaust.

turbulence: Mixing or swirling fluid flow.

turbulent boundary layer: A boundary layer which mixes and swirls.

V

velocity: A measure of how fast an object moves; calculated by dividing the distance traveled by the time it takes to travel the distance.

vent: A hole.

viscosity: A measure of how much a fluid will resist flowing across a surface.

volume: A measure of how much space is inside an object.

vortex: Rotating fluid flow that resembles a whirlwind.

W

wake: The region of flow separation which extends past the surface of an object.

wave drag (for aeronautics): One of the four types of drag caused by the interactions of shock waves over the vehicle and the pressure losses due to the shocks. Wave drag can also occur at transonic or supersonic speeds.

weight: A force equal to mass multiplied by the acceleration of gravity.

wind tunnel: Chamber where gas (usually air) is blown over an object to calculate its aerodynamic forces, like lift and drag.

wing warping: Technique used by the Wright brothers to twist the wings of their airplane allowing control of the vehicle.

X-planes: Experimental aircraft.

Y

yaw: One of the three axes of motion for an aircraft; yaw moves the nose of the aircraft side to side.

yoke: A control mechanism in an aircraft, which resembles a car steering wheel, used to roll the wings.

REFERENCES

Alexander, R. McNeill; Locomotion of Animals, Blackie and Son Limited, 1982.

Alexander, R. McNeill; Dynamics of Dinosaurs and Other Extinct Giants, Columbia University Press, 1989.

Allen, Glover Morrill; Bats; Dover Publications, Inc., New York, 1939.

The American Heritage Illustrated Encyclopedic Dictionary, Houghton Mifflin Company, Boston, 1987.

Anderson, John D., Jr.; Fundamentals of Aerodynamics, 3rd Ed., McGraw-Hill Book Company, 1984.

Anderson, John D., Jr.; Introduction to Flight, 3rd Ed., McGraw-Hill Book Company, 1989.

Angelucci, Enzo; World Encycleopedia of Civil Aircraft, Arnoldo Mondadori Editore S p.A., Milano, Italy, 1981, Crown Publishers, New York, 1982.

Archbold, Rick; Hindenburg, an Illustrated History, Warner Communications, 1994.

Bach, Richard; Biplane, Harper & Row, 1966.

Balibar, Francoise and Maury, Jan-Pierre; How Things Fly; New York, Barron's Educational Services, 1987.

Ballif, Jae R. and Dibble, William E ; Physics: Fundamentals and Frontiers; New York, John Wiley and Sons, Inc., 1972.

Bakker, Robert T.; The Dinosaur Heresies, Zebra Books, 1986.

Benford, Timothy B. and Wilkes, Brian; The Space Program Quiz and Fact Book, Harper & Row, Publishers, New York, 1985.

Bergaust, Erik; Illustrated Space Encyclopedia, G.P. Putnam's Sons, New York, 1965.

Berliner, Don; Before The Wright Brothers; Minneapolis, Minn., Lerner Publications Co., 1990.

Bilstein, Roger E.; Flight in America 1900-1983, The Johns Hopkins University Press, 1984.

Borelli, Giovanni Alfonso; On the Movement of Animals, Springer-Verlag, Germany, 198l.

Botting, Douglas; The Giant Airships, Time-Life Books, Inc., 1981.

Braybrook, Ray; The Aircraft Encyclopedia, Simon and Schuster, Kingfisher Books, Ltd., 1985.

Cole, Joanna; A Bird's Body; New York, William, Morrow, and Company, 1982.

The Concise Columbia Encyclopedia, Columbia University Press, New York, 1995.

Corbett, Scott; What Makes A Plane Fly?; Boston, Little, Brown, and Company, 1967.

Cousteau, Jacques; The Ocean World of Jacques Cousteau—The Art of Motion, World Publishing Company, New York, 1973.

Cromer, Richard; The Miracle Of Flight; Garden City, New York, Doubleday and Co., Inc., 1968.

Dean, Anabel; Bats—the Night Fliers, Lerner Publications Company, Minneapolis, MN, 1974.

Eide, Arvid R., Jenison, Roland D., Mashaw, Lane H., and Northup, Larry L.; Engineering Fundamentals And Problem Solving, 3rd Ed., McGraw-Hill, 1997.

Ethell, Jeffrey L.; Smithsonian Frontiers of Flight, Smithsonian Institute, 1992.

Eyewitness Visual Dictionaries, The Visual Dictionary of Flight, Dorling Kindersley, Inc., 1992.

Fleisher, Paul; Secrets of The Universe; New York, Anthenum, 1987.

Helmericks, Harmon; The Last of the Bush Pilots, Alfred A. Knopf, New York, 1977.

Hill, John E. and Smith James D.; Bats—A Natural History, University of Texas Press, Austin, TX, 1986.

Hill, Philip and Peterson, Carl; Mechanics and Thermodynamics of Propulsion, 2nd Edition, Addison-Wesley Publishing Company, Inc., 1992.

Hopf, Alice L.; Bats, Dodd Mead &, Company, New York, 1985.

Horner, John R. and Lessem, Don; The Complete T. rex, Simon & Schuster, 1993.

Hoyle, Geoffrey; Flight, Ladybird Books, Loughborough, 1994.

How Things Work, Planes Gliders, Helicopters and other Flying Machines, Kingfisher Books, 1993.

Hylander, Clarence J.; Feathers and Flight; New York, MacMillan Co., 1959.

Jablonski, Edward; Man Without Wings, Doubleday and Co., Garden City, New York, 1980.

Jackson, Donald Dale; The Aeronauts, Time-Life Books, Inc., 1980.

Knight; Clayton; The Story Of Flight; New York, Grosset and Dunlap Publishers, 1954.

Laycock, George; Bats In the Night, Time-Life Books, New York, 1995

Lemmon, Robert S.; All About Birds; New York, Random House, 1955.

Levenson, Elaine; Teaching Children About Science; New York, Prentice Hall, 1985.

Loftin, Laurence K.; Quest for Performance—The Evolution of Modern Aircraft, National Aeronautics Space Administration, 1985.

Lopez, Donald; Flight; Alexandria, VA., Time-Life Books, 1995.

The Lore of Flight; Mallard Press, New York, 1971, Rev. 1990.

Macquitty, Miranda; Eyewitness Books—Shark, Dorling Kindersley Limited, 1992.

Markle, Sandra; Outside and Inside Birds; New York, Bradbury Press, MacMillan Publishing Co., 1994.

Massey, David; Airline Pilot, Future Aviation Professional of America, 1990.

Matthews, Peter; The Guinness Book of Records, 1995 Edition, Bantam Books, New York, 1995.

Matthews, Rupert; Record Breakers of the Air, Troll Associates, Mahwah, 1990.

Maurer, Richard; Airborne; New York, Simon and Schuster, Inc., 1990.

McGowan, Christopher; Dinosaurs, Spitfires, and Sea Dragons, Harvard University Press, 1991.

Moolman, Valerie; The Road to Kitty Hawk, Time-Life Books, Inc. 1980.

Nevin, David; The Pathfinders, Time-Life Books., Inc. 1980.

Nitske, W. Robert; The Zeppelin Story, Cranbury, New Jersey, 1977.

Oates, Gordon C.; Aerothermodynamics of Gas Turbine and Rocket Propulsion, American Institute of Aeronautics and Astronautics, Inc., New York, New York, 1984.

Parke, Robert B.; America's Flying Book, Ziff-Davis Publishing Company, 1972.

Parker, Steve; Eyewitness Books—Fish, Dorling Kindersley Limited, 1990.

Patent, Dorothy Hinshaw; Feathers; New York, Cobblehill Books, Dutton Children's Books, 1992.

Perkins, Otho; Physical Science; Englewood Cliffs, New Jersey, Globe Book Co., Inc., 1987.

Peterson, Houston; See Them Flying, Air-Age Scrapbook, 1909-1910, Richard W. Baron, New York, 1969.

Peterson, Roger Tory; The Birds; New York, Time-Life Books, 1967.

Peterson, Russell; Silently, By Night, McGraw-Hill Book Company, New York, 1964.

Physics Today; Chicago, World Book, Inc., 1986.

Prendergast, Curtis; The First Aviators, Time-Life Books, 1981.

Rosen, Seymour; Understanding Forces Physics Workshop-2; New York, Globe Book Co., 1983.

Schober, Wilfried; The Lives of Bats, Arco Publishing, Inc., New York, 1984.

Seeley, H.G.; Dragons of the Air, An account of extinct flying reptiles, Dover Publications, Inc. 1967.

Selsam, Millicent E. and Hunt, Joyce; A First Look at Bats, Walker and Company, New York, 1991.

Shevell, Richard S.; Fundamentals of Flight, 2nd Ed., Prentice Hall, 1989.

Simon, Hilda; Feathers, Plain and Fancy; New York, The Viking Press, 1969.

Stever, H. Guyford and Haggerty, James J.; Flight; New York, Time Inc., 1965.

Van Deventer, C.N.; An Introduction to General Aeronautics, America Technical Society, 1970.

Videler, John J.; Fish Swimming, Chapman and Hall, London, 1993.

Wohl, Robert; A Passion for Wings, Aviation and the Western Imagination, 1908-1918, Yale University Press, New Haven and London, 1994.

The World Book Encyclopedia; Chicago, World Book Inc., 1986.

Zisfein, Melvin B.; Flight, A Panorama of Aviation; New York, Pantheon Books, Random House, Inc., 1981.

INDEX